RAWGE JONES

And There I Was... JUST MINDING MY OWN BUSINESS

BUSINESS

A HYBRID MEMOIR

Grateful Acknowledgments to My Amazing Friends

I want to extend my heartfelt appreciation to Karen, Bernie, Chris, Rene, and my wonderful wife Rhonda. You all took my rambling thoughts and managed to transform them into a book!

Contents

Preface

Sharing stories has always been a passion of mine, especially those from my own life.

For years, my wife and I hosted a monthly old-time Gospel music concert. Those concerts grew into a regular Gospel Show, with raucous music, delicious BBQ food, and a time for my humorous stories.

But the Pandemic came along and changed everything. Suddenly, we had no concerts and I had no audience. Then, to shake things up even more, I spent all of April, 2020, in a hospital. For a time, I was on a ventilator and my situation looked grim.

I had taken creative writing classes in college, over 35 years ago. Back then, I had dreamed of someday writing a book. The Pandemic and my time in the hospital rearranged my timelines. All of the dreams that I had saved for "someday" suddenly became things that I needed to do now. I came within a few heartbeats of running out of "somedays."

Shortly after I was released from the hospital, I started writing and sharing thoughts each week, on social media. This book was born out of that year of writing.

I'm no longer waiting for "someday."

Someday is today!

* * *

For more true short stories, follow me on social media.
Rawge the Wannabe Writer

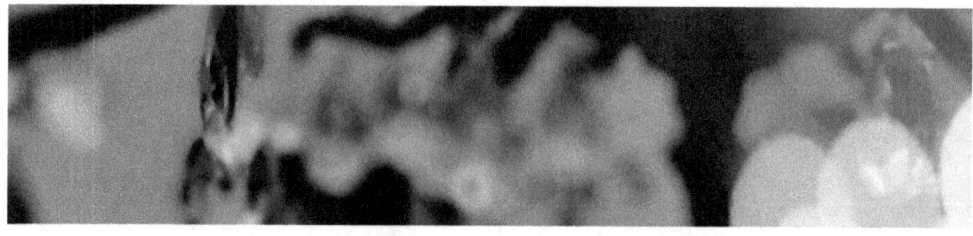

POINT OF LIGHT

1

POINT OF LIGHT

The 1960s, in the rural areas of California's central San Joaquin Valley, may be the most UN-understood time in the history of our nation. No one seems to study it. No one seems to care about it. No one even references it. It was a time-period that *was*, and then it *was not*, and then everyone just moved on. It was a brief shadow in our geographic history with too many shiny spots around it to draw anyone's waning attention. If not for the short-handled hoe, Cesar Chavez, and a few other temporal icons, the whole time and place would be without interest. But it's a time I remember. It's when and where I grew up.

During the great Dust Bowl migration, millions of poor farmers and others left the plains states and headed west. Almost a quarter of a million of them poured into California, seeking work and a new life. Though these hardworking people were not greeted with open arms, they forged through hardships and poverty and settled into California farm life. For the next 30 years, they would drag their families along in beat-up cars and trucks, camp on the sides of the roads, and move throughout the state to nurture, grow, and then pick its fruit and vegetables. These sun-wrinkled and leathery people were my grandparents and parents. These were my people.

Though no one cares, the 1960s were a distinctly pivotal time of transition for these middle-America expats. That period witnessed the once-wandering dust bowl migrants pass the shovel, hoe, and knife to the new workforce of immigrant Mexicans. The migrant working whites had mostly found their place in California economics and settled into permanent jobs, leaving the immigrant Mexicans to take over the brunt of the demanding farm work. This cultural and socio-economic shift happened in the span of one decade, and almost no one even noticed.

I remember the time pretty well. For me as a child, the sun rose out of a cotton field, beat down on us all day and then set into another cotton field. Tomorrow, it did the same thing. When it wasn't hot and dusty, it was rainy and muddy. The beautiful Spring season lasted about a week and Fall seemed even shorter. My farming dad spent his days trying to stay a step ahead of the calamities of weather and nature. My mom spent her days working random jobs off the farm and still trying to keep up the full-time duties of mother, wife, and matriarch. We were poor, just like everyone around us, so no one really noticed it much.

Looking back, it seems that our little community was such an isolated spot. Every adult person thought alike and acted alike. Everyone worked the same basic jobs and made about the same basic money. Everyone had the same gripes, fears, and dreams. Everyone spoke the same, cussed the same and expected the same. Very little influence came into our town and even less went out. Despite the major changes taking place around us, none of the people I knew seemed to change much. If they did, it was at a glacier's pace, and again, no one noticed.

I've tried many times to think back as far as I can. I have fleeting memories of moments when I was very young. I don't know if they are real or not, as most of them are just flashes of time. I can recall a gift that a kid gave me in the first grade. I can remember getting to walk around with my new shoes on in kindergarten, while the other kids sat in a circle and sang the new shoes song. New shoes were rare enough at the time that it was a minor celebration when any of us poor kids wore them to school. I remember that. I remember my two older sisters taking care of me and running out to pick me up every time I stepped barefooted into a goat-head sticker patch and burst into tears. I remember that well.

But my earliest real memory is of bedtime when I was probably a little less than five years old. We lived in a small shotgun house on a farm, nestled between a 2-story barracks and other farm housing at Wood Ranch. Only a few years before, the clutter of houses were known as Camp 16. These farm labor camps had evolved just enough to no longer be called simply by their number and now each had a name more palatable to its settled white community. It was far nicer to introduce yourself at church or school and tell someone that you lived at Wood's Ranch. Camp 16, at least in name, was a thing of the past. Times, they were a-changin'!

Shotgun houses like ours got their name from a joke. It was said that if you fired a shotgun through the front door, the bullets would pass cleanly through the house and go straight out the back door. These houses were small, cramped, and cheaply made. Much of ours was made from pieces of other houses and every one of the inside doors was a little bit too short, so when they were closed, there was an odd gap at the top.

Our little house had two bedrooms. Mom and dad had one bedroom and all four of us kids slept in the other. My brother Steve and I slept in a bunk bed, while my two older sisters shared a small bed on the opposite side of the room. Steve was still a toddler, so he got the safer bed on the bottom, while I climbed into the top bunk each night.

This was a time when people lived in fear of their monthly "light bill," so any unnecessary lights were always turned off. Nights got dark, both indoors and out. Outside, you could still see the Milky Way and its seemingly infinite number of stars. But inside, it would just get dark.

When we were all lying in bed and mom clicked off the light switch, for a minute or so you genuinely couldn't see your hand in front of your face. I can remember lying in bed and staring toward the black ceiling. I could usually hear the little black and white TV in the living room, and sometimes a hint of light crept in through the little gap above the door. My earliest memory in life was when I lay in bed, with my head in exactly the right position, I could see a tiny speck of light straight above my spot on the top bunk. If I moved an inch to the right or left, it disappeared. My brothers and sisters couldn't see it when I asked them about it, and they didn't believe that I could see it. So, it was special to me, and I fell asleep each night looking at it.

At the time, with my budding little scientist's brain, I speculated that it was somehow a star showing through the ceiling. I inspected the ceiling during the daylight but could find no hole or other possibility for the light. Our house was rickety and rundown, but it did have a roof and ceiling, so there was no way for a star to show through. I wondered if it were something miraculous and somehow related to an angel watching down on me. Each night, I stared at it, pondered its mystery, and appreciated its company in the dark.

Twenty-five years later I saw the tiny speck of light again. I was a student at the University of California at Davis. I was attending an undergraduate physics class in 26-Wellman Hall, one of the smaller lecture halls on campus. The hall is the basement of a five-story building and had no windows. On the first day of class, I arrived early to ensure I got a back seat near the door. I sat down in the dark room to wait. As I slumped in the theater-style seat, I laid my head back and stared at the dark ceiling. There it was again, that tiny speck of light. If I moved my head in either direction, it disappeared. It was the same speck of light from my childhood.

I stared at the tiny speck and recalled those nights in my little bed. I chuckled at the thought that here I am in a college physics class and still have no idea why there is a tiny star on the ceiling. For the rest of the quarter, I arrived at that class early to sit and stare at the minuscule dot on the ceiling. When the other students would arrive and the lights would get turned on, it would disappear.

I saw the light again about 25 years later. This time, I learned the secret to its existence. My wife and I belonged to a small church in our neighborhood. We played music and did a host of other jobs necessary in a church that never has enough volunteers. We were doing some work on the building, and I had gone there at night to take some measurements of the small sanctuary. When I was finished, I shut off the lights and the sanctuary fell dark. As I was about to lock the doors, I realized that I had left my little notepad on a chair towards the back row of seats. I was very familiar with the sanctuary and could maneuver around the seats in the dark. I found the notebook in the last seat in the back row and decided to sit in the dark and soak in the peace and silence for a moment. It had been a long day and I reveled in the solitude. My eyes looked around the darkness at the faint and barely recognizable shapes; the gathers on the black stage curtains, the pillars and speakers, the silhouette of my guitar against the back wall.

As I looked around the dark ceiling, there it was again. The tiny speck of light was back and this time it was even brighter than I had ever seen it! I slid to the next chair, and it was gone. I moved back and it reappeared. I tested it by leaning to the right and then to the left. With each movement, it would be gone, but it would be back the moment my eyes got into the perfect spot.

This time, though, I didn't sit and ponder. I calculated as close as possible to where it was located on the ceiling and went to turn the lights on. I walked to the point directly beneath and stared at the ceiling. Nothing. I walked circles to look from every angle, but still nothing. I walked over and opened one door to allow a small amount of light in, turned the lights off again and went back to my seat. There it was again. With the small amount of light coming through the door, I could better pinpoint its location. I made my mental notes and turned the lights on. I walked to the location and scanned the ceiling, but still saw nothing but aging white paint and ceiling texture.

There was a big ladder in the next room, so I wasn't giving up. I dragged the unwieldy ladder into place and climbed high up to a dangerous point that allowed me a closer look at the ceiling. Even at close examination, the texture looked and felt no different than any spot in the rest of the room. Still, I wasn't ready to give up. I crawled down and grabbed a flashlight from the soundboard drawer, cut the lights, and again climbed back up the ladder. The moment I pointed the beam to the ceiling, there it was. I leaned in and was surprised to see that a tiny piece of glitter had somehow gotten stuck to the ceiling paint. That's it. No wormhole through the time-space continuum. No star. No miracle. Nothing but a tiny shred of reflective plastic the size of a grain of sand.

I put the ladder back into the foyer and put all the chairs back into their perfect rows. I turned off the lights and sat back down to stare and ponder the little speck of light. Although I was a bit let down that the answer wasn't something more grandiose, I still rather marveled that something so small could reflect that much light. As I sat there in the dark, in deep thought about the properties of light and childhood and college years and myself, I felt somewhat convicted. If a tiny piece of plastic the size of an ant's head could reflect enough light to capture my attention and make me drag around a 14' ladder in the dark, then what is expected of my ability to reflect light? Surely, a lot is expected of 200 pounds of walking, talking, thinking human being.

As I sat there in the dark, one thought led to another (and another and another). I quietly vowed to reflect more light. I would be brighter. I would try harder to be light, especially when everything around me seemed dark. I would be that glimmer that someone sees when they're slumped in the back row or the light that a poor kid sees in the dark. I would see all the light in my life and reflect it to the rest of the world.

Just before I got up to leave, I faintly chuckled at God. What a master! He played the long game on me. He helped me see a speck of light when I was five years old, then let it work on my mind for fifty years, before letting it be a life-changing moment... in a little country church sanctuary... in the dark... in the back row... and without a preacher in sight.

* * *

POINT OF LIGHT

A BORDER STORY

2

A BORDER STORY

She knew in her heart, if she could just make it to the border and cross over, it would mean a new life. There would be jobs and work. She could find housing and put food on the table. Her three kids could have shoes and clothes and attend school. The border was opportunity.

It would be a long journey—over a thousand miles. Her husband was in prison, but she would travel with her disabled brother and his wife. They were more fortunate than many. They had a car and everything they owned was packed inside and on top. They would sleep on the sides of the road and stop to work any odd jobs along the way. With prayers and crossed fingers, they left their homeland.

They had heard stories of the land of milk and honey. But they had heard other stories, too. They had heard of people being turned away or beaten at the border. They had heard of news articles describing the migrants as rapists, murderers, and thieves. The stories told that the children were filthy, infected with diseases, and covered in lice. The writers of those articles went on to say that the invaders crossing the border checkpoint were only there to lie, cheat and steal. There were other articles warning the residents that everyone coming in was there for welfare, and if not, then they were there to steal the locals' jobs.

The journey was long, well over a month. The old car broke down several times and they slowly sold their belongings to buy parts. Many times, there were helpful strangers with tools and water and sometimes with food. Of course, there were others that looked only to take what little they had. But they moved on, and forward, with the border always on their minds.

It was midnight and dark when they crossed through the border checkpoint. The little group and others drove on through Tehachapi and were in Bakersfield at sunrise. Before them lay the entirety of the great San Joaquin Valley. Before them lay opportunity.

That was my mom's story. As a child, she and her brothers, my Grannie and her brother and sister-in-law, all arrived here in the 1930s. They left an Indian reservation in Oklahoma to venture to California. My dad and my paternal grandparents made a similar trip from Arkansas.

Mom and I talked about that journey a lot. In the years before she died, I would drive home from Davis after my last college class let out. I would usually get to Avenal late in the evening and Mom and I would often talk the rest of the night. Mom was a deep thinker. We talked about the difference between migrants and immigrants. We discussed how both groups were searching for a better life, but the immigrants had to cross a national border to find it.

It was during one of those deep conversations that Mom introduced me to the notion of white privilege, well before that even became a term. Mom was almost 60 and slowly dying. One night she told me that everything she had (and it wasn't a lot) - a two bedroom one bath house, a car, and health insurance - was the result of three things. A life of hard work and sacrifice, being born white, and being born in the USA. She mentioned that there were many others willing to work hard and sacrifice, but without the other two blessings. Well, she was glad she had them.

My mom and her brothers, my Granny, my Uncle Sun and his wife, all found what they had come for. They worked. They traveled up and down California's Great Central Valley, picking fruit and vegetables, hoeing cotton, and anything else they could find to turn muscle and sweat into pay. My Dad, his brothers, and my Papa and Grandma did the same, from Buttonwillow in the south to Marysville in the north, then back again.

Ten years after the border crossing, Mom and Dad found each other on a farm. It wasn't too long before they got married in Reno, and then settled on a farm in the tiny town of Huron. A year later, my oldest sister came along. Maybe the struggles were still fresh, but her middle name is Hope. Maybe it just sounded pretty. But maybe it was homage to all that the border crossing had to offer.

I've read most every book about the Dust Bowl migration, from the classics like the *Grapes of Wrath* to newer books like *American Exodus.* I've read the old news articles that called the "Okies" and "Arkies" refugees. I've stared at Dorothea Lang's haunting picture of the *Migrant Mother* and saw my family in her worried face.

I'm thankful that I have the blood of these hard-working and brave people in my veins. I'm grateful that my poor mama taught me to cherish all that I have. I'm thankful to know my history as I form my thoughts on our southern border and the people arriving there each day, seeking a better life. Maybe some of them will name their first daughter Esperanza.

I'm thankful that the land of opportunity is big.

* * *

WHAT'S IN A NAME

My Name
is
RAWGE

3

WHAT'S IN A NAME

When I was in the second grade and really just learning to read, I couldn't get enough reading material. I made frequent trips to the town's library, but I read everything that I could get into my sight – road signs, food wrappers, advertising literature and junk mail. Occasionally I'd get my hands on the holy grail of literature, the local newspaper.

Our family didn't subscribe to a single newspaper, but once in a while I'd find an old copy of the weekly paper that they threw for free in town people's yards. We didn't get these out on the ranch, so when us kids were bumming around town, I'd scour the front yards at vacant houses. If I was lucky, there'd be several strewn about the overgrown grass. I'd pick each one up, dust off the grass and bugs and stick the little rolled-up bundles into my back pocket.

Each evening, I would unroll the mess of weathered brown paper and flatten them on the kitchen table. Cereal boxes were good reading, but the newspaper was *real* reading. After I had read all of the cheesy articles about old ladies and their quilts, drunks that got arrested, and various people getting awards, I would start reading the want ads. I'd read about people selling all kinds of stuff. I'd read about jobs that were available and about houses for rent. One evening, under a section called "Legal Notices," I saw an ad that read:

NOTICE OF PETITION FOR CHANGE OF NAME

Henceforth, John W. Smith shall be known as William W. Johnson.

I read the words, but I couldn't understand what it was about. I asked my mom, and she told me that occasionally people would change their names and that to make it legal, the name changes had to be published in the newspaper. Once it was in the paper, people would know about it and know what to call them.

As often happens when you absorb yourself in reading, you're bound to encounter a revelation now and then. I had no idea that someone could change their name! I had never been overly fond of my name. I answered to Rog, which was short for Roger. There was another farm kid named Roger and he was a little older than me. So, he got the long version. I answered to the short version.

In school, as we were learning how to use a dictionary and the pronunciation guide for each word, one of our assignments was to write our name with the phonetic spelling. Along with that, we were to write a short description, just like we would see in the dictionary. We would get extra points for using as many three-syllable or larger words as possible. My example looked like this:

Rog [Raw·ge] - A good boy who buys stuff from magazines and will someday travel to Mississippi. He likes to read the encyclopedia. When he is grown up, he will go to the university and become a veterinarian or an agronomist or a biologist or a politician in the House of Representatives.

Well, I got a few points knocked off because the pronunciation guide wasn't quite right, but I had a lot of long words. As I looked the assignment paper over with my big "A" on the top, I stared at the word Raw·ge. It seemed exotic and a little mysterious. It was far better than the boring Roger. That assignment really clinched the way I'd spell my name for the rest of my life, and I started using it. My reluctant teachers finally just gave in to me signing my work as Rawge. I'm sure that they were just picking their battles and I had plenty of others for them to fight. Soon, Rawge showed up on books, balls, baseball gloves, and anywhere else that I needed to show my ownership.

A few days after I read the *name change* article, my mom found me sitting at the table with a pencil and paper. She glanced over and asked me what I was writing. I responded I was writing to the newspaper to change my name. I told her, "Henceforth I will be known as Rawge Ralph Richard B.R. Billy-Bob Bivis Jones."

Of course, mom was a bit shocked and asked why in the world would I ever want to change my beautiful name? I told her that I just wanted to do it for fun. But I lied. I had a deeper motive.

Needless to say, I didn't get a name change.

But here's the deal. Even though I was a sweet kid, angelic even, I did occasionally cross some lines. I've mentioned that everyone called me Rog except when I was in trouble. We all know what it means when your mom says your whole first name. We also know what it means when mom says your first and middle name. Well at my house, when mom said ROGER DALE JONES! it meant I better cut and run 'cuz a whoopin' was just about to happen. My mom was fast. She could catch me in 10 steps and cut a switch off a tree on the way.

So, I figured if my mom had to say Rawge Ralph Richard B.R. Billy-Bob Bivis Jones, those few extra words might just give me that precious one second head start in the race to outrun the switch!

So later in school when I read William Shakespeare asking so eloquently "What's in a name?", I'd likely exclaim, "A few extra steps ahead of your ma! That's what's in a name!"

* * *

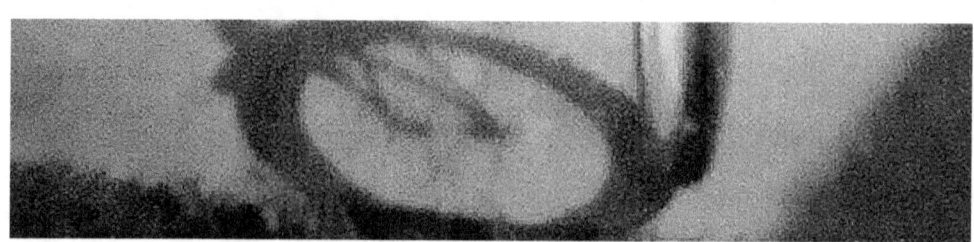

ONCE UPON A TIME...

4

ONCE UPON A TIME...

Once upon a time...

Yep. You're already intrigued and ready for a delightful story because you heard those romantic and magical words, "*Once upon a time.*" Don't fall for it! The word ONCE is the most dangerous word in the human vocabulary.

That word is responsible for all manner of grief and pain in this world. That single syllable word is responsible for a lot of pain in my life. It's certainly responsible for the biggest and most visible scar on my body. I got it a long time ago. The incident involved me, my brother, a few farm kids, my brand-new Sting Ray bike, a piece of plywood and a few two-by-fours. As I'm sure you've already imagined, we were setting up a ramp and jumping over various objects. Keep in mind, this was all happening during the heyday of Evel Knievel, the most famous daredevil that ever lived. Knievel used a motorcycle to jump buses and cars and other big things. To add an even greater element of danger, he would jump things that were on fire.

We kids didn't dare light something on fire, but after a few small jumps, we had no problem eyeing a stack of rolled up rusty barbed wire. Yep, jumping a stack of barbed wire would add just the perfect amount of danger to the stunt. At first, I resisted and claimed it was too dangerous. I even resisted when they chided that Evel Knievel would be ashamed of me.

"No way! I don't care! I'm not doing it!"

But then I heard the magic words, "Come on Rawge, we'll just try it *once*." Apparently adding the word ONCE in there completely changed things in my mind. My healthy skepticism of danger was gone. Before I could even say "Hold my root beer," I peddled hard and hit the ramp. As expected, I sailed a few feet in the air and safely landed to a boisterous round of hoots and hollers. I skidded to a stop, caught my breath and it was done. I was ready to head home and revel in the accomplishment of my daring feat. Evel Knievel would have been proud.

But even before the dust settled, I heard the only words that are possibly more dangerous than once .... the words "ONCE MORE!"

Those two words may be even more dangerous because they hold within them the idea that the first time turned out fine, so "once more" will surely be even finer. Well again, hearing that word ONCE managed to disarm my healthy fears. I got my bike ready and headed for the ramp. But this time the two-by-fours fell over at the last minute, and I piled, full speed, into the small mountain of barbed wire! I shiver to this day just to write about the painful wreck. My little ten-year-old body was covered in tiny spots of blood and one big gash down the middle of my back. That four-inch scar down my spine still loves to remind me of my foolishness.

So, friends, listen to me. Beware of the romantic word "ONCE" and its evil cousin, "ONCE MORE." There isn't a notion in this world that is more dangerous than "I'll only do it *once*," or "I'll only do it *once more*." Throughout the world, from emergency rooms to twelve-step programs, there are countless people, like myself, that were lulled in by the siren's call.

Once. Once more. Once upon a time.

* * *

ONCE UPON A TIME...

RIDING THE RAILS

5

RIDING THE RAILS

From the day we are born, certain things are in place to protect us. For adults, there are laws, barricades, and orange cones. For kids, there are rules and signs, locked gates and fences. There are designated safe places where you can run a bit wild, but always under a watchful eye. There are some neighbors that would quickly tattle if they saw you doing something wrong or dangerous, and then there's extended family that would snatch you up and paddle you like you were their own kid.

But even with all that in place, on some days all of these safeguards fall apart, and adventurous kids do dumb stuff. I remember one of those days.

One year, I raised a kid goat from a bottle, and, thus, it thought I was its mother. So, unless I could sneak around and lose it, "Ajax" followed me everywhere I went. The goat and my knee-high brown mutt, Chico, were like shadows. Wherever I went, they followed.

It was a perfect summer morning. Everything felt right to just sit on one of the half-buried tires that my dad had planted in the yard, side by side, in an effort to make a fence. The tires were ugly, even by our Okie standards, but they served to create a boundary when my dad said, "Stay in the yard." On this particular day, I had no instructions, stated or implied. The day was wide open as I sat with my daydreams.

And there I was just minding my own business, when my younger brother Steve came out of the house with two dimes in his hand. He suggested we walk to the farm's shop and get a soda from the Coke machine. We headed to the far end of the ranch yard, which consisted of five little houses, some sheds, a two-story barracks for the big influx of workers during harvest seasons, and an outdoor bathroom with showers for those workers.

The Coke machine was in the shop at the end of the ranch yard. The shop was a curved-top tin building that had been dragged over by a tractor from the surplus sale at the nearby Lemoore Naval Air Station. It sat on three-foot-high cinder block walls and had a concrete floor. The shop contained the typical array of shop tools – a big air gun and black sockets, an air compressor, and a welding machine. The entire place and most every tool were covered in grease and oil. This was where my Papa Myron worked on all of the farm's equipment. Every time we approached the shop, he'd always greet us with the same grandpa line and a laugh, "You boys keeping out of trouble?"

When we got there, we were surprised to find the shop empty. Even walking past the other houses, the whole farm seemed to be oddly deserted. With no one around and no dust coming down any of the four dirt roads that led to the shop, we decided to play mechanics for a while.

As Steve swung a sledgehammer, smashing something on a big blacksmith's anvil, I practiced my arc-welding. I grabbed the welding hood and turned on the huge welding machine. I snugged the helmet tight on my forehead, put a rod into the electrode, clicked my chin down so that the hood fell over my eyes, and started welding.

Like any novice welder, the rod stuck to the metal a few times and had to be shaken off, but within a few tries I was laying a weld-bead on the metal table like a pro. For future bragging rights, I decided to weld my initials into the table. I hadn't completed the R when the rod got so short that the molten hot metal splatter was burning my arms. But that didn't stop me. With a jerk of my head, I threw the helmet back so that I could see, grabbed a pair of big leather welding gloves and went back to work. I finished the sloppy J and stepped back to admire my work. I'm sure it looked like a big bird had crapped on the table, but if I looked at it just right, I could see a capital R and a capital J. I was sure I was the best ten-year-old welder in all of Fresno County!

I took my gear off and then checked again for dust coming down the roads.

Nothing. We were still alone, just me, Steve, a dog, and a goat. As I was chipping the slag off my new welding work with a little hammer, just like I'd seen my dad and uncle do many times, I heard my name from behind. I snapped around and was greeted by three other kids from the farm.

You never know when there's a snitch in the crowd, so Steve and I both played it cool and told them we were there to buy a Coke. We asked them if they had any money. They all fumbled in their pockets, and each pulled out a few coins. Pennies didn't count because the machine wouldn't take them. Among the five of us, we had 40 cents in dimes and nickels. Since there wasn't enough for each of us to get a soda, the smart thing would have been to scrounge up an empty bottle, wash it out at the water hose, and then share. If we poured out just a little of the four bottles we could afford, we could easily fill up a fifth bottle. But that's the kind of thinking that you do when adults are around. In our unguarded situation, there was surely a better answer than that!

My brother was gifted with an uncanny ability to think outside the box. To Steve, rules were always gray. Within seconds, he proposed that we walk the few miles into town and try the ancient Coke machine at the old gas station. It was worn out and had the potential of giving you a Coke AND your money back in the return slot if you put your dime in and then hit the coin return at precisely the right moment. It was a masterful idea, so off we went.

Getting to town was a pretty good walk, and of course, we were not supposed to do it without express permission. We didn't have permission but hadn't exactly been told not to either. Another gray area.

To get there, we'd walk a few miles of dirt roads, and then follow some railroad tracks until we reached the melon-packing sheds at the edge of town. From there, we'd have to walk past some houses and then walk a few blocks more down the little main street, but surely five kids, a dog, and a goat wouldn't stick out and raise any concern!

When we got to the railroad tracks, we were all surprised to see a train sitting on it about a half-mile in the direction opposite town. By that time in the end of the 1960s, the tracks were almost abandoned, and I had only seen a train on it a few times. Even without a train on it, we were strictly forbidden to walk on the tracks or even get near the tracks. Under penalty of a serious whooping, we were to never get closer than the dirt road that paralleled the tracks.

Again, my gifted brother's brain started to work, and he threw out the idea of walking to the train, jumping into one of the cars, and riding it into town. My fearful side kicked in, and I told everyone it was a bad idea. I covered my hesitancy by pointing out that it was at least a half mile in the wrong direction and probably wasn't even going into town if it even moved again at all. My ever arguing, but quick-witted little brother countered with the fact that it was pointed in the right direction, and he could hear its engine idling. Steve and the other kids headed in the train's direction while Chico and Ajax just stared at me to see what we were going to do. With no danger signs posted anywhere, no fences, and no dust coming up the road to save me, I trotted to catch up with the other kids.

As we got up to the train, the engine was idling. From a distance, we had seen some men standing in the shade on the side of the engine car. Grain tanks and elevators were located nearby, so the men were surely waiting while some grain cars filled with barley. We crouched and walked gingerly by on the side opposite the men. Even the dog and goat were on their best behaviors and never made a sound.

We had walked past about forty or more rail cars, but they were all closed-up. I half-hoped we couldn't find an open car and would have to give up, but sure enough, my brother pointed ahead and then made a shush sign with his finger on his lips. We got to the open car, and he climbed in. I picked up my goat and then my dog and hoisted them in, after which my brother grabbed my hand and pulled me up. He and I grabbed the other's arms, and as Steve yelled, "All Aboard!" we yanked the last kid in.

At the suddenness of Steve losing his mind and yelling like a conductor, we all got wide-eyed and nervous that we'd be caught. But before we could even imagine the angry men running for the rail car, the train lurched and knocked us back onto the floor. In another second, it was moving ahead and picking up speed. Within a couple of minutes, we were riding the rails and headed for town!

We picked ourselves up from the floor and tried to steady our feet. Steve let out a whoop and stood in the middle of the car with his arms out and feet apart like he was surfing. It looked so fun that everyone started doing it and belting out a Beach Boy's tune. The dog went to the open door and stuck his head out looking up the road like dogs do when riding in a car. The goat just stood in the middle of the car, rocking from leg to leg as the motion shifted us around.

I moved to the back of the car so that I could see through the door into the distance. We all knew that at some point we'd have to jump out. On the way to the train, we had already discussed the dismount. One kid said that he'd heard from an older kid that it was easy. All you had to do was run in the direction opposite of what the train was traveling, and jump. He claimed that the two speeds would cancel each other out and that it would be just as easy as stepping off a school bus.

We had traveled a couple of miles and were nearing town. The group were still scattered around, pretending to surf, and I was still all the way in the back, fretting about the impending need to jump. The goat was standing in the middle of the car, and the dog still had his shoulder against the door, face in the wind and his wiggling tail sticking out with joy.

As I watched the whole scene, passing from character to character, my gaze froze on the goat. I saw a look in its eyes that I instantly recognized. I knew it well and panic covered my face. I started yelling, "The goat! The goat! Grab Ajax! Somebody grab him!" The others were all just feet from the white animal, but not one of them moved. Before I could get another word out of my mouth or a step in the goat's direction, it stood on its hind legs and bounced toward the poor dog's hind-end. The two were friends, but the sight of that jiggling tail and unguarded butt was just too much of a tempting target. The goat's head and little curved horns hit the unsuspecting dog with such force, it sent him somersaulting through the open door and off the speeding train. I screamed profanities at the other kids for just watching it happen. When I stumbled my way to the door, I could still see poor Chico tumbling in the dust and being left behind by the traveling train.

In a panic, I ran and grabbed the goat and lifted it into my arms. Still screaming and venting my anger, I ran in the opposite direction of the train, and jumped, clinging to the older kid's idea that the two speeds would cancel each other out for an easy landing.

Well, the kid was wrong. Completely wrong. As I screamed my last foul word, we hit the ground and bounced like we had been shot out of a cannon. For a few seconds, I was rolling while the goat was skidding in front of me. The next thing I knew, I passed the goat and it was skidding behind me. Then we were both just tangled up together and tumbling down the dirt road. We finally skidded to a stop in the dust.

I sat there for a few seconds and listened to the fading clickety-clack of the disappearing train. For a moment, dust and dirt covered my face and I couldn't see. As the faint tears slowly cleared my eyes, I took stock of our condition. The goat jumped up, shook, and seemed almost unfazed. I stood up and looked at my arms and legs. I shook each arm and then each leg. I opened and closed each hand and shook my fingers. Nothing was broken. I had some scrapes here and there, on my arms and face, but I had gotten far worse from mere bicycle wrecks.

Just when I thought it was a miracle that I wasn't really injured, I spit out a big glob of blood. And then another. And then blood just oozed out of my mouth into the ground below. I could taste the blood and now could start to feel the pain. I wiped my hand on my shirt and put my finger in my mouth. My teeth were fine, but somewhere during the wreck and all my name-calling, I had managed to seriously bite my own tongue, which wasn't exactly dangling out of my mouth, but was swollen, bleeding, and hurting more by the second.

As I was still probing my tongue with my finger to try and assess the damage, I remembered why I had jumped. Oh no! Chico! I turned to run back to where the dog had fallen, but there he came, running at wide-open speed. He reached me and ran circles around my legs, tail wagging and just as happy to see me as I was to see him. He didn't even appear to be holding any outward grudges toward the goat. After a couple of minutes of our happy reunion, we all started walking toward town to investigate the fate of the other rail-riding kids.

After just a few hundred steps, a big concrete pipe stood on the side of the road with a farmer's well water flowing out of it. I washed my face and arms. Then, the dog, goat, and I all got a drink. There was a tree with some white buckets sitting under it, left behind by some farm workers eating their lunch.

I looked up and down the road but saw no dust or trucks in any direction. I was too tired and sore to go on. I just needed a short rest, so I sat down.

I sat for a while with my mind running through all the events of the day. I had my finger in my mouth, still poking around on my tongue, when I heard some voices. I looked up and saw my companions, hurrying up the road in my direction, waving and laughing.

They were certainly happy to see that none of us were dead. They were all drinking a soda. When they reached me, my brother pulled a bottle out of his back pocket and handed it to me. They all blabbered to tell me how the train went on and then stopped in town. They easily hopped off about a block from the little gas station. They ran over and managed to cheat the wobbly Coke machine out of a bottle, bought four more, and then hurried back in my direction.

I popped the lid off the Coke bottle using my hand and the lip of a piece of metal sticking out from the farmer's well. I took a big drink and screamed from the sudden pain of the spicy drink on the open gash in my tongue. I used my finger to pull my lip down and stuck my tongue out to show them the wound. As I started to tell them all that had happened, they busted out in laughter. My tongue was so swollen that they couldn't understand a single word I said. I sounded like I was talking with a mouth full of marshmallows.

Through his laughter, my brother said, "Come on, mush mouth. Let's go before Dad starts looking for us."

As we walked along the road, we got back to the spot where the goat and I had hit the ground. There were marks all over where we rolled and tumbled, as well as big mouthfuls of red blood which I spit and dripped on the ground. We all stood there for a moment, staring at the ground, and silently remembering the whole ordeal. It was in that quiet, thought-filled moment that my brother said what might have been the most profound statement in his entire life.

"Damn Rawge! You would have been fine if you'd of just kept your big mouth shut!"

We all laughed.

He was right. In all my yelling and cursing and blaming, I had managed to just about bite my tongue off. But that's what we do when we're angry. We yell and blame and curse. If I'd had just kept my mouth shut, I would have gotten off with only a few scrapes.

There have been many times in my life since then when there were no signs or fences or people to save me from myself. There were no guards or laws or written rules. There were no societal barricades or social orange cones, and my mouth got me in trouble. But I have learned, truly, a whole lot of potential trouble can be avoided by that simple thought from years ago. Sometimes in life, the best thing to do is just keep your mouth shut.

That train still ran a few times after that day. I have a flattened buffalo nickel that Steve and I put on the tracks one time just ahead of the train. It's flat and smooth and every time I see it, I'm reminded of those days with Steve and a lesson learned about keeping my mouth shut.

Thank you, Brother.

* * *

THE 60 WATT CROSS

6

THE 60 WATT CROSS

One day when I was about seven years old, I was sitting in class with Reverend Briles, the Sunday school teacher at our little church. He was also Head Pastor, Associate Pastor, Youth Pastor, Church Groundskeeper, and our little town's only plumber. It was a really small church! The reverend told us kids that he had a glow-in-the-dark plastic cross that he would give to the first kid to memorize the books of the Bible. He opened the box and showed it to us. It was off-white plastic and really wasn't much to look at. Seeing the lack of interest by the dozen or so kids in the class, he decided to make it dark in the room so that we could get the full effect. The reverend closed the shutters on the windows and then, in a *ta-da* moment, switched off the lights. The room fell dark and the little cross glowed a cool faint green. For the next thirty seconds, as our eyes became accustomed to the darkness, the cross was the only thing visible in the room. In that moment, I vowed that I'd win that beautiful cross!

On the drive back to our farm, I started to work at it. "Genesis, Exodus, Leviticus..." I repeated over and over in the car. "Numbers, Deuteronomy, Joshua, Judges, Ruth..." I repeated it as I lay in bed that night. I continued to study those words at every waking moment. I worked on it at school recess and lunch, and all the way home on the long bus ride. I worked on it in bed until late at night. I had a pretty good mind for stuff like that and within just a couple of days, I had it all committed to memory. Half the time I couldn't remember to take my books to school, but with the right incentive, I had memorized sixty-six ancient book names in two days.

After school on Wednesday, I begged my mom to take me to the pastor's house. If I was forced to wait until Sunday, I just knew that some other kid might jump in and win the cross before I had a chance to rattle off my new words. My mom wasn't about to bother the busy pastor in the middle of the week, but she assured me there was little chance of someone usurping my opportunity.

On Sunday morning I raced into the little Sunday school room and announced that I was ready to recite the books and claim the glowing cross. The pastor was a little startled that someone was ready to try it the first week, but he gave me a shot. So, I took a big breath and spewed out sixty-six words so fast that I would have been the envy of every auctioneer in America. I guess that I never missed a word because I left there that day with the little plastic cross.

As soon as I got home, I drove a nail in the wall across from my bed and hung the little cross against the fading white paint. I closed my curtains and door to make the room as dark as it could get. Well, the pastor hadn't pulled a parlor trick. The cross glowed in the dark just like it did in the little Sunday school room! I laid down on my bed and stared at the plastic symbol for some time, letting the books of the Bible rattle around in my head. I went through them one by one. Then I wondered if I could say them backwards. I struggled with that for a bit and then decided that they weren't supposed to be used that way, since it was pretty much impossible to say it all backwards. But as I lay there wondering about the Bible, mostly wondering things like why they didn't just put the books in alphabetical order, I noticed that the glowing cross had started to fade. Soon, it wasn't even visible.

Well, for all the delights of having a green glowing cross on my wall, there was a downside. The glow just didn't last long enough. But being the clever kid that I was, I quickly figured out that I could take it down and lay it across the top of my lampshade, turn the light on, and it would recharge. So that became my pattern. For the next few weeks, I alternately moved it from the wall to the lampshade and back to watch it glow. I'm sure that my hard-working dad wondered why the power bill ticked up and my mom shook her head each time she passed by my room and had to reach in and click the light off.

I had a wonderful time with the cross until one fateful day. Before I went out to play, I had placed the cross in the usual position on the lampshade. The moment I switched on the light, I heard a pop and it went dark. The bulb had blown out. I unscrewed the bulb and looked at it. Sixty watts. Surely, we have one somewhere in the house. I scrounged through every cabinet and drawer, but there wasn't a bulb anywhere. Where earlier I was a clever kid, now I needed to get downright sneaky. I went out to the garage and took a look at my dad's work bench. He also had a lamp. With almost no hesitation, I unscrewed the bulb from his lamp and quickly replaced it with my bulb. Surely, he'd just think that it had blown out and go buy a new bulb to replace it. No one would be hurt.

When I got back to my room and started to screw in the purloined bulb, I noticed that it was a 100-watt bulb! I was giddy to think that if my old 60-watt bulb made the cross glow, then it would absolutely shine like a beacon after spending some time with a 100-watt bulb! I put everything back together and got it ready for the evening. It was wintertime and it got dark early. As soon as Mom called us kids to dinner, I would run by my room and switch the light on.

At the end of the day, I stuck to my plan. That evening I ate my dinner with the anticipation of seeing the cross shining like a sun that's been charged by a 100-watt light bulb. Dinner time was typical for our small family. Dad talked about struggles on our ranch while Mom talked about struggles to pay the bills. My two sisters talked to each other, and Steve and I did the same. As the conversations went on, and somewhere between "please pass me the potatoes" and "did you boys feed the dog?", I smelled something odd.

At first it was just a whiff and hardly noticeable over every other aroma in a farming family's house. But within a couple of minutes there was no denying the sickening smell of burning plastic. My dad looked around and said, "What the hell is that smell?" At that moment, I KNEW! I jumped up from the table and said "Oh nooooo!" and raced around the corner to my room.

Apparently, the new 100-watt bulb was a whole lot hotter than the scrawny old bulb I had been using to charge up my cross. At some time during dinner, the cross had melted enough to fall through the lampshade and land on the bulb. I screamed in horror at the sight of my once beautiful jade colored cross melted into a smoking black glob and dripping from the hot light bulb. I screamed, burst into tears and fell to my knees, just as my panicked mom ran into the room. I am sure that from all my screaming and wailing, she must have thought I had just cut a finger off or broken my neck as I had rounded the corner of the hall. She grabbed me up into her arms and was yelling, "What's wrong? What's wrong? What's wrong?"

"I melted the cross! I melted the cross!" I screamed as the giant tears rolled off my face. I cried with the weight of a kid that had just committed a most terrible sin and was surely destined to spend his eternity in hell. Maybe even longer! My mom looked towards the smoking lamp and realized what had happened. She got a bit of a smile on her face with the relief of knowing I still had all my fingers and limbs. She held me tight for a long time and did what moms do. She softly whispered "It's ok. It's ok. It's ok. Just stop crying for a minute." After my sobbing slowed down, she sat me down on the bed and talked about the cross. She explained to me that the melted cross was just a piece of plastic and that the hope and love that it symbolized was all that mattered. She assured me that I would not go to hell over a moment of childish carelessness. I felt better and calmed down.

That night, I lay in a dark room with no glowing cross. With clinched hands, I said my "Now I lay me down to sleep" prayers and closed my eyes. I lay there with the peace of knowing that a kid won't go to hell over doing stupid stuff.

I fell asleep hoping that stealing your dad's light bulb would also get a pass under the same youthful indiscretion clause.

* * *

Day Old Chicks
25 for $**1**⁹⁰

Standard Quality   Light Mixed Breed

More Poultry Dollars with Wards Chicks

Priced at big savings! Live delivery and satisfaction guaranteed. All breeders blood-tested by Stained Antigen Method or Agglutination Tube Test for Bacillary White Diarrhea. For Easy Payments see Ward General Catalog. **Superior Quality.** They have better appearance, score higher and have longer breeding and heavier laying ability. From carefully culled and inspected pure breed flocks. **State variety wanted.** *Shipped from Hatchery.* **Postpaid.**

287 PK 4101	25 Chicks	50 Chicks	100 Chicks	500 Chicks
Leghorns	$2.55	$4.65	$9.25	$45.75
Barred Rocks	2.69	5.15	9.75	48.25
S. C. Rhode Island Reds	2.69	5.15	9.75	48.25
Buff Orpingtons	2.75	5.25	10.00	49.50
Minorcas	2.69	5.15	9.75	48.25
White Wyandottes	2.75	5.25	10.00	49.50
Light Mixed Breeds	2.50	4.75	9.00	44.50
Heavy Mixed Breeds	2.55	5.00	9.50	47.00

Standard Chicks. Fine chicks of high grading and quality from vigorous healthy flocks and well known hatcheries with a reputation for hatching quality chicks. *Shipped Direct from Hatchery.* **Postpaid.**

287 PK 4100	25 Chicks	50 Chicks	100 Chicks	500 Chicks
Leghorns	$1.98	$3.68	$7.25	$35.75
Barred Rocks	2.20	4.15	7.75	38.25
Rhode Island Reds	2.20	4.15	7.75	38.25
Buff Orpingtons	2.25	4.25	8.00	39.50
Minorcas	2.20	4.15	7.75	38.25
White Wyandottes	2.25	4.25	8.00	39.50
Light Mixed Breeds	1.90	3.75	7.00	34.50
Heavy Mixed Breeds	2.15	4.00	7.50	37.00

Prices Subject to Change Without Notice.

COCK-A-DOODLE DOOOOO!

7

COCK-A-DOODLE-DOOOOO!

The sun was just hinting at rising with a few rays glowing through the curtainless window in the little bedroom I shared with Steve, my younger brother. I was startled awake and looked over to see him standing on the bed, thumbs tucked under his armpits, crowing like a rooster.

"Cock-a-doodle-dooooo!"

"Steve! What the heck are you doing?" I whispered. "Get down! You're gonna wake up Mom and Dad!"

My brother motioned for me to shut up, and started crowing again, but this time even louder.

"Cock-a-doodle-doooooooooo! Cock-a-doodle-doooooooooooooo!"

I lay in bed, quiet, tilting my ear toward our parent's bedroom. I was just waiting for my dad's heavy footsteps to come stomping down the hall to see why his crazy son was crowing at the top of his lungs at sunrise. I sat quietly, and Steve stood waiting. Seconds passed with nothing, so he did it again. But this time, he did it even louder and longer.

"Cock-a-doodle-doooooooooooooooooooooooooooooooooooooooo!"

Again, the whole house fell silent. Steve never had a lot of sense, but at that moment, I thought he had surely lost what little he had. I heard mom and dad's bed creak and waited for the footsteps. Nothing. But then mom's voice shouted from down the hall.

"OK! I get it! Go back to sleep!"

I was puzzled. What the heck just happened? One moment I'm dreaming on a peaceful Saturday morning, and the next moment my crazy brother is strutting on the bed and crowing like a rooster. Steve looked at me with a big grin.

"You watch, we'll get hamburgers today!" he stated, proudly.

Then it all made sense, but it's a long story...

I appreciate that if I want something today, I can grab my phone, open an app, buy it, and expect to have it at my door tomorrow. The Amazon truck rolls into our driveway just about every day. We get grocery deliveries at least once a week. We get dinner delivered from nearby restaurants. We can even get a case of champagne or wine dropped off at the front door on a regular basis. We complain that Big Brother and Big Data follow our every move, but I say it's a small price to pay to have a mimosa on Saturday morning after you only realized that you were fresh out of Prosecco the night before.

Of course, if you are more than fifteen years old, you know that this was not always the case. Growing up on a ranch in the middle of nowhere, our shopping opportunities were pretty thin. If you were a kid with a dollar bill burning a hole in your pocket, you had to just let it burn and wait for the bi-weekly trip into town. Some weeks, the trip was just a short jaunt into our nearest town, which had no spending possibilities for a kid other than a soda and candy bar. But other times, we traveled farther to a larger town that had a mall. There, a kid could blow through a dollar pretty quickly and actually come home with something. But even then, it was a long wait.

When I was about ten, I learned of another option. Mail order. We didn't know it at the time, but mail order was the precursor to Amazon Prime. All the major stores had catalogs to browse through. The catalogs showed the items, the price, and a nice picture to lure you in. There were blue electric guitars and amps. There were portable radios and bulky walkie-talkies. There were fishing poles and tackle boxes. There were pages and pages devoted to toys. These three-inch-thick catalogs had almost anything a kid could want. Almost. I found that even at the tender age of ten, I had some exotic tastes that Sears and his brother Roebuck just couldn't provide. I liked animals.

Sometimes when we were in town, I would drop into the barber shop, a cool old place with three big spinning barber chairs in the middle and a twirling red, white, and blue barber sign in front. I didn't like the barber much because he was rough and shaved my head even when I lied and told him that my mom said to only take a little off the top. But I played nice and treated him with respect every time I dropped in.

"Good morning Mr. Raymond! Nice to see you. How's business? Hey, you got any old hunting magazines that I could take home?"

Usually, Mr. Raymond had a few dog-eared *Field and Stream* or *Outdoor Life* magazines that had already been read by every farmer in town. With just a little pleading and some kind words from me, he'd let me grab a couple, roll them up, and stick them in my pocket.

Once I got home and was sitting in my bedroom, I'd unroll the magazines, flatten them out, and let the *real* shopping begin! The bulk of the magazines were devoted to articles about famous fishing and hunting locations. Florida for tarpon. Montana for rainbow trout. Colorado for big mule deer. There was always a "How-To" section to teach you how to be a better fisherman and a "true life" section where people wrote in about how they almost got eaten by a bear or bitten by a giant rattlesnake. I enjoyed reading it all, but the back three pages are what lured me in.

The back pages were all advertisements. Quarter page ads lured rich people into booking guided hunting trips for elk and moose. Some ads had pictures of men holding up ten-pound bass. Those first pages of ads were a paradise for rich people. But if you turned just one more page, that was where my interest landed: *Animals For Sale.*

"Darling Pet Monkey. Makes an adorable pet. Almost Human. Eats same food as you. Even likes lollipops! $18.95. Check or money order. Shipped by airmail to your nearest post office."

"Live Pet Seahorse – With Free Seashells – $1"

"Chinchilla pair. Start your own fur farm. Also, Great Pets – $12"

There were ads for foot-long baby alligators, big lizards, and chameleons. One company offered a small plastic incubator with six free quail eggs and big letters that stated, "SEE THE MIRACLE OF BIRTH. Only $6."

Sitting here fifty years later, I am embarrassed to say I had a monkey and an alligator and most everything else. But on this particular day, I saw a new ad.

"500 one-day-old baby chicks. $16. Lay eggs in only 5 months. Accredited Stock. Start your own business. Guaranteed live delivery."

Ten seconds after reading the ad, I knew that the color-changing chameleon would have to wait. I wanted to become a chicken farmer!

It's easy to see from the ads that these items weren't something that could ease the pain of a dollar burning a hole in your pocket. These items cost real money. Most farm kids rarely had two nickels at the same time. Minimum wage in 1969 was $1.60 an hour. But farm wages were excluded. The government kept out of the business of telling farmers what they had to pay for their child or illegal immigrant labor. A hardworking grown man might only get a dollar an hour, so a scrawny kid was in trouble if he set his sights on something with a $16 price tag. I don't care how many A's you brought home on the report card for a dime a piece, if you wanted something more than a box of Cracker Jacks, then you'd better get a jar and start saving.

I wasn't much of a saver, or a worker, but there were other ways to make a buck. I was enterprising and usually had a side hustle or two going on, raising and selling farm animals. I had raised and sold everything from pigs to peacocks. I always managed to have a coffee-can bank account hidden away from my parents. But during this particular spring, I was the richest kid in the county. I had come into the princely sum of $100, and I got it the old-fashioned way, sports gambling!

Every farmer in our area loved baseball. Most every adult and half the kids listened on the radio to every game. On weekends, we watched the games on little TV sets and then talked about them at every conversation. Everyone had their favorite team, like the Giants or the Dodgers, and it was especially fun when your team was playing a friend's team.

Each fall, every adult man's conversation was about the World Series. Who would make it? Player's stats. Injured players. Fastballs and bull pens. Home runs and RBIs and other statistical stuff. I didn't collect baseball cards and really cared very little about the details of it. But I cared about the World Series. For all the misplaced hype, it had something I did anticipate. It had the World Series pool.

As soon as the playoffs were completed and the National and American leagues had their winners, someone would start drawing lines on a paper to create one-hundred squares, and then start selling squares. When you "bought a square," you chose one and wrote your name in it. Once all the squares were filled, numbers between 0 and 9 were drawn and then written along the X and Y axis. American league was on the left, and National league was along the bottom. If the final score was 6-4, then you used your finger to trace up to the 6, and then slide over until the number below was a 4. Whoever had their name in that square was the winner.

Some of the pools cost a nickel. If you won, you'd get $5. Most pools were a quarter, but some required as much as a dollar. The dollar pools gave the winner $100. A dollar-a-square pool was big money, and I just happened to have a dollar burning a hole in my pocket. I considered splitting my dollar up and increasing my odds by getting into several smaller pools, but $5 or even $25, just didn't sing to me like the crisp song of a $100 bill. I liked all our founding fathers, but I had a tender spot for the portly Benjamin Franklin and his grin on the green one hundred.

My uncle Chuck had organized a $100 pool. I wanted in, but I had some questions. If I won, would I be able to keep all the money? He said that he'd pay it all, but I'd have to talk with my dad about keeping it. I asked if there was a chance for a tie? Nope. I asked where he would keep the money in case he had to go to a hospital or to war? It's all handled. I asked if it was legal? He replied that it was perfectly legal if you're older than 18 years old. He then asked me how technical I wanted to be about the legalities? He ended with asking whether I was in or out? I told him I'd need to think about it. He told me to hurry because when the squares are gone, that's it!

I was ready to jump in, but I really wanted to talk to my dad. I wanted to know that if I won, I'd get to keep all the money and spend it as I pleased. If Dad was planning on keeping a bunch of the money, then I'd be better off playing a couple of smaller games and hoping that he didn't hear about them. So, I decided that I'd just ask him, but I'd wait until I caught him in a good mood.

For whatever reason, farm, spousal relationship, financial, or something else, Pops wasn't in a good mood much. Most days, I didn't even see him until he was home from work well after dark. Then, I'd be in bed by the time he had a few beers and wound down. But I caught him on a Saturday as he was driving by in his pickup. I stopped my bike and waved him over to the side of the road. He nodded at me, and I just jumped in with the question.

"Hey, Dad, I've got a dollar that I got from Papa Kinley and Grandma for my birthday."

(I lied. There's no way I'd have ever kept a dollar for seven months, but it sounded good.)

"I want to get in on a baseball pool. If I won, could I keep all the money?"

He looked at me for a moment and then started being fatherly. I hated it when he was fatherly.

"You know you won't win, right? It's a one in a hundred chance. It's about the same as flipping a coin seven times, and getting all heads, every time. Have you ever done that before?"

I answered that I didn't think it had ever happened before. But the odds didn't dissuade me, so I just stared at him.

"But I guess if you want to throw your money away, then buy a square. If you win, you can keep the money. But you ain't gonna win. You'd be better off spending it on Cokes in town, but it's your money."

He ended by telling me that I'd better go find Charles because he thought the pool was already full.

Well, shit, I didn't see that coming. I had the dollar deep in my pocket. I started my bike toward the shop with my fingers crossed, hoping that Uncle Chuck would be there and that the card wasn't full. As I rounded that last farmhouse, I could see my uncle's familiar service truck parked at the shop. I skidded up and exclaimed to anyone that could hear, "I want to buy a square!"

Uncle Chuck stepped back from under the hood of a greasy tractor.

"Well, you just made it Rawge, there's one square left."

He pointed toward a square piece of cardboard sitting on a welding table. It had penciled lines and names written in each square. I saw names I recognized and names that I didn't know. There was one blank square toward the top left.

"Dang! I don't even get to pick my own square?"

"Nope, not when you wait for the last day. Maybe it's lucky!"

"It is lucky. That's why all these other losers skipped it!"

We both laughed, and I wrote my name in capital letters—RAWGE.

A short week later, it was game time. After the numbers were drawn, I had Mets-4 and Orioles-1. All the men were gathered around the TV with a beer in one hand and a cigarette in the other. Several mentioned that I had good numbers. Excitement was in the air. I played around outside with my brother and some cousins but walked over every time I thought about it to check the score.

Before long, I got involved with the cousins and lost track of time. We had ventured off to parts unknown and it was getting dark. I told them that I needed to get back to the house because I might be rich. They were all bored with whatever we were doing, and we all ambled back toward our houses.

When I got back to the house and walked up to the porch, Uncle Chuck had a big grin on his face. He stretched out an old GoJo soap can toward me and said, "Here you go, Money Bags! You won!" Everyone laughed. Even my dad laughed and made some comments, showing the results of a six-pack or two. I stared at the can and thought, yep, I just tossed a coin and got seven heads in a row.

The moment I got into my room, I dumped the contents onto my bed. There were quarters and dollar bills, fives and tens, and even a couple of twenties. I stacked the bills in piles and counted every penny to see if Dad had kept his word. There was exactly $100. To most, it would look like a pile of money. For me, it looked like opportunity.

The following week, I discovered my new side hustle. Chicken farming. I did just as I had for every other of my mail-order transactions. I took my money to the post office after school and bought a money order, an envelope, and a stamp. I stood at a counter that had ink pens hanging on a chain, and I filled out my name and address. I stuffed everything into the envelope, licked it and closed it, and applied my stamp. I dropped it into the "out of town" slot and started the grueling wait. Two weeks for shipping and handling were always the saddest words I'd ever read.

While I waited, I prepared my chicken farm. I built a big pen with wire that I had pulled off a beaten-up cotton trailer. I put a tarp roof on it to keep out rain and chicken hawks and installed a plywood door with a piece of a tire for a hinge. I added a big upside-down hubcap for water. I figured that I could just sprinkle food on the ground, so that the cute little chicks could learn to find food once they were grown and on their own. I bought a big bag of chick food at the feed store and got to tell everyone inside about my big chicken order. It was all planned. Now, I had to wait just thirteen more days for the precious cargo to arrive.

I don't know how someone can ship a box full of baby chicks across the country. But they did. I went by the post office every day after school but was told each day that nothing had arrived for me. On a Saturday, my mom got a phone call from the man at the post office telling her that I had a package, and it was making noise and it stunk. Mom got in the car and spent ten minutes looking for me. She knew from experience that unless she knew where I was, she could have driven around for hours without finding me. So being the wonderful mom that she was, she drove into town alone and picked up my chickens. Two boxes of them.

That evening, when I finally walked up to the porch, mom was standing there with her hands on her hips.

"Your crying baby chicks are in your crying baby chick pen," she stated.

"Oh Mama, you got them? I love you!"

I gave her a big hug and ran toward my pen. I pulled out my pocketknife and cut the boxes open. I'll never forget the sight of all those tiny white chicks packed tightly in the box. I took them out, handfuls at a time, and placed them on the ground. They hopped and staggered around for a bit and seemed to greatly appreciate the water. They pecked around at the piles of ground-up baby chick food. They all cheeped and chirped and acted pretty happy, not even seeming to hold a grudge for being taken from their mama, stuffed in a box, and flown halfway across the country. They had food, water, a pen, and a kid to pet them. Life was good.

Just as the advertisement had promised, the chicks grew quickly. But after they stopped being cute and fuzzy, my interest in being a chicken farmer waned a bit. By the time they were a couple of months old, it was far easier on me to just let them be "free-range" chickens and convince them to mostly fend for themselves. I'd just go outside each day or so and holler, "Here, chickychickychicky," while I tossed out a few handfuls of food. They were always hungry. A bug or an errant weed seed didn't have a chance around our place with 500 starving teen-aged chickens running around.

By the time the chickens were five or six months old, I had built a place for them to lay eggs. I would attempt to herd as many as possible into the little chicken shed each evening. The shed had bins and old tires full of straw. Even though most of the chicks turned out to be roosters, there were still a lot of hens. I was excited when I found the first egg. Then there were five. Then there were 20. Then there were A LOT of eggs.

Even though I collected the eggs from the egg shed, many of the chickens laid eggs hidden around our farm. I would always be surprised by seeing a clucking hen with a brood of chicks, having no idea where she may have made a nest and sat on the eggs for three weeks without being discovered.

I collected eggs every day, but I never sold any. My family and everyone we knew ate them. I never sold any roosters, but we and everyone else ate them too. My granny taught me how to kill and clean a rooster. After the first ten or so, I didn't have any problems with chopping off a young rooster's head, pulling out its guts, and plucking all of its feathers. I cleaned pheasants and fish too when we had them, but I drew the line with anything that had four legs. That was too much for me.

Farming is always a cycle of feast or famine. One year we'd make money and eat well, the next year we didn't and learned to eat a little lower on the hog. Some years, if the famine stuck around, there's no hog. And no cow. And not much of anything else. That was 1969, the year of my chicken venture. We didn't have a hog or a cow, but, dang, did we have chickens!

We woke up in the morning and had eggs for breakfast. We had egg salad sandwiches on white bread for lunch. For dinner, it was fried chicken. The next night it was BBQ chicken. The next night it was grilled chicken. Before long, Steve and I would joke, "Hmmm. I wonder what we're having for dinner tonight?"

"Let me think," Steve would say, tapping his chin with his finger. "I'm gonna guess, COLD DEAD CHICKEN!"

We'd have a good laugh. Each night we'd wait for the plate to hit the table to see what manner of chicken mom had devised. Steve would look at it and smile with a smart-assed grin, "Oh Mom, that looks delicious, what is it?" Mom wouldn't dignify his disingenuous complement with an answer. At her silence, he'd say, "Well, whatever it is, it looks delicious." The cavalcade of chicken and egg dishes went on for a couple of months.

One evening, as Steve, Dad, and I were sitting at the dinner table, waiting for mom to unveil the evening's meal, Steve quipped into the air, "If the pan has a chicken or an egg in it, I swear that I'm gonna turn into a chicken!"

Instantly, Dad snapped back, "What did you say?" He had his angry look on his face.

Undeterred, Steve had the nerve to repeat it, word for word.

Then I saw it coming, Dad started with his fatherly talk again. He told Steve how fortunate he was to have chicken. Then, he said some stuff about kids in Africa. He told Steve that he was more than welcome to skip dinner if he was worried about growing feathers. He went on about how hard Mom worked and how disrespectful it was for him to complain. I just kept quiet. But the whole mess blew over when Mom came in and sat a pan on the table.

As the pan came around, we each used our spoon to ladle it onto our plates. As Steve slung the food from his spoon to his plate, I watched him quietly mouth the words, "Cold Dead Chicken." He was as fearless as he was dumb. Dad apparently saw him mouth the words, too. He slung his hand up and pointed. "Get your ass in your room!" I silently prayed that Steve could pull off the next 30 steps without doing anything to make it worse.

Steve was asleep by the time I got into the room. I laid down in the dark and said my prayers. I said them like we were taught, giving thanks to God for filling our needs. I gave thanks for family and friends, I gave thanks for a roof over our heads, and I gave thanks for school and teachers. I gave thanks for chickens and that we had food to eat. I prayed for mom and dad. I ended my prayer by asking God to watch over Steve and to help keep him out of trouble. I finished with an "Amen" and then a second "Amen" for emphasis.

I woke up the next morning with Steve crowing like a rooster. Mom understood his signal. Dad never said a word, and for lunch we had fried bologna sandwiches and then pork chops for dinner. The chicken streak was broken.

I don't know if it was the second "Amen," but I still do that on those certain prayers. To this day, I still hate chicken. And to this day, when I do eat it, I start by shaking my head and smiling...Cold Dead Chicken!

* * *

SPEED

8

SPEED

Light travels at 299 million meters per second. I've seen it. That's pretty fast!

Electricity travels in a wire at over a million kilometers per hour. I've been shocked. That's pretty fast!

Mark Twain once said that a lie can go around the world three times before the truth can get its shoes tied. I've seen it happen on Facebook. That's pretty fast!

Steve Earl sang a song that his first pistol was a cap and ball Colt. It shoots as fast as lightnin' but it loads a might slow. I've shot one. That's pretty fast.

Bruce Lee could jab a foe in the throat six times, while they blinked. I saw the movie. That's pretty fast!

Usain Bolt ran a top speed of 27.33 mph. That's over 40 feet per second. I watched the Olympics. That's pretty fast!

So, what's the fastest thing I've ever seen? The back of Mom's hand when she told me something and my eleven year-old self accidentally responded by saying "Bullshit!" I never saw it coming. OK, now that's fast!

* * *

PAPA KINLEY

9

PAPA KINLEY

As I was growing up, my Papa Kinley was a model for what a grandpa should be. He was gentle, kind, and he had the patience of a glacier. He taught me many things, including guitar. He was a fiddle player but knew the basics on several other instruments. I'd sit with him and play chords on my cheap guitar while he fiddled the melodies of old fiddle tunes. When I would play a messy G-run and end it in an open B instead of an open G, he would just fiddle a quick *shave-and-a-haircut* in B, so my goof didn't sound as stupid. Then we'd both have a good laugh.

Papa Kinley was born in the rural mountains of Arkansas. He made his living as a fur trapper during winter and as a mule team operator during the rest of the year. As mules were replaced by tractors, he adapted and could operate and repair most any piece of farm machinery.

During the Great Depression, when much of the country's farmers and laborers found themselves hungry and out of work, he and Grandma Elsie moved to California. Papa quickly found work in the farming country of the San Joaquin Valley. There were no fur animals to trap in the flat agricultural lands, but he told me stories and taught me how to use chicken wire and metal coat hangers to catch pigeons and an occasional pheasant. He taught me how to identify every animal on our farm by their tracks left in the dusty roads.

Papa was also empathetic and wise. He always listened when I talked and explained anything I asked. No question was out of bounds. Even as a kid, I saw qualities in him that I didn't see in others. He was a man of his word. If he told me that tomorrow we would go fishing or walking or anything else, I knew that I could count on it. I didn't have to worry about hearing "Sorry, I got busy." Papa counted me as important as any other person on Earth.

I remember when he told me that he had cancer and was going to die. I was devastated by the news. He let me cry for a few minutes before he said that we could spend the rest of his time just being sad, or, since he felt good that day, we could enjoy it. He had a smile on his face, and it won the moment.

I was at his house that day because it was a holiday and I didn't have school. We ended up getting in his car and driving to Hanford to go to the Monday Sale, a popular swap meet. After we prowled around all the junk, we walked over to the little livestock area. That was my favorite spot. There were always chickens and pigeons, rabbits and other animals for sale. I immediately put my eyes on the most beautiful chicken that I had ever seen. It was a golden rooster, with a long sleek tail. I had a lot of chickens, but this one was just incredible. Papa ended up buying it for me and we put it into a doubled-up big paper sack.

When I got home, I couldn't wait to turn it loose into our yard with the rest of my chickens. I had chickens of most every size and color, but none of them had the beauty of this new rooster. I was sure that every other chicken would just bow down to the new golden-robed king of the barnyard. I opened the bag and the rooster jumped out, hit the ground running, and never looked back. It ran across our yard, through the horse pasture, through the shop yard, and disappeared into a cotton field. I screamed and chased it, but it ran like a wild animal and flew even better.

Well, as it turned out, it wasn't a golden chicken rooster, it was a golden pheasant rooster, and it was wild.

A few days later, I was driving around the ranch with my dad in his pickup. As we rounded a corner, I saw my prized golden rooster out in a freshly plowed field with about 100 wild ring-necked pheasants. All of the dark, burgundy colored pheasants stood out from the bare soil, but the beautiful gold color of "my" pheasant was stunning in the morning sun.

I jumped out of the truck and took off after it. But just like all the other pheasants, it ran for a few steps, jumped into the air and disappeared a half a mile away. As I crawled back into the truck, my dad chuckled at my futility. "Yep, it's wild" he said with a grin. But I wasn't ready to accept that glaring fact.

From then on, my life's mission was to recapture that pheasant. I was angry. It wasn't fair. We bought it, it was mine, and it should just walk around our barnyard and let me look at it.

I built a trap, larger than my pigeon traps, and then spent the next several weeks chasing the wild rooster. Each day, before and after school, I'd drag the big wire trap around to different corners of the fields. But wherever I put the trap, I would see the pheasant in the opposite corner of the field when I went back to check. This aggravation went on for several weeks and getting that pheasant back was all that I could think about. I thought about it at school and used my precious white paper to sketch out new trap ideas. On the school bus, while the other kids laughed and joked with one another, I sat back with my eyes closed, thinking about that rooster. I planned for the way I would put it in a pen after I captured it. A few weeks in solitaire and I was sure it would see the error of its feral ways. All I needed to do was recapture it. I slept each night with wistful dreams about the golden chanticleer.

Soon pheasant hunting season rolled around. We would have hunters come from all over California. Many of them were rich people with fancy guns, fancy clothes, and fancy dogs. I put the word out that no one was to shoot the golden pheasant. But after the season closed, I never saw the beautiful bird again. I'm sure it's hanging on some rich man's wall.

Now that I've had fifty years to think about it, I'd be willing to bet that Papa Kinley knew he'd hidden a message in there for me. It's taken five decades, but I know it now. Chasing that wild pheasant took a couple of months off my life that I'll never get back. I spent that time being angry and thinking that life wasn't fair. I plotted and cursed and worried and stressed. But I could have spent that time enjoying the beauty of that pheasant, even if from afar. The same way I enjoy birds now. I could have been happy every time I came around the corner and saw it out in the field, sitting up on a big dirt clod. I could have smiled when I watched it beat its wings and crow. But I didn't. I wasted my time being angry.

Then and now, life pretty much isn't fair and it's easy to feel unhappy, unsatisfied, and cheated.

A happy life comes from letting some things just pass, learning from them, and then concentrating on enjoying the beauty in every day you have. Yep, every day.

Thank you, Papa Kinley!

* * *

PAPA KINLEY

DIRTY JOKES

10

DIRTY JOKES

Every teenage farm boy had a dirty mouth. It was always a balancing act to remember your audience. You didn't dare risk a slip when speaking to your parents, other parents, or a teacher. A tongue slip of a "shit", or "damn", or God forbid, an "F" bomb in the wrong company and a boy would find himself reeling from a slap that seemed to come out of nowhere. Or worse, sitting with a bar of soap in his mouth.

Foul mouthed teenage farm boys knew about ten jokes. We could only remember ten, because our brains hadn't yet fully developed. At that age, our brains were ten percent gray matter and ninety percent testosterone. All the jokes were dirty, sexist, racist, or all of the above. We all knew the same ten, but occasionally a new one would find its way in. Somehow or other, most of them found their way in through my brother, and he just couldn't wait to share it.

"Hey, Rawge, you know all those red cows over by Uncle Herbert's?"

"Ya, they're Herefords."

"Ya, whatever they are. That guy bought a bull for $1,000. He put it in the pasture, and it wouldn't screw a single cow. It just stood there. But he called that vet from over in Hanford, and he came out and gave it a big pill. That bull jumped up and ran over and screwed every cow. Then it wouldn't stop. It headed for the goats and started trying to break in with the horses!"

"Damn! What was in the pill?"

"I don't know, but it kinda tastes like cinnamon, and it's hard to get the taste out of your mouth. I need some water!"

Yep, I got to hear that one 157 more times that year, every time we saw a damn cow.

* * *

GALLO DEL DIABLO

11

GALLO DEL DIABLO

Growing up a farm boy in the proverbial middle of nowhere, we had very few rules that we had to follow. As scant as they were, we still managed to break the few we had on a regular basis. We knew the boundaries, but just couldn't help but push the limits. Without fail, at some point, we'd cross the line and a whooping was in order.

Dad's whoopins were worse than Mom's, but neither of them rose to an "OH my gawd, someone call CPS!" moment. Mom's were shorter, but more intense, while dad's seemed to drag on for a bit longer. My brother and I had developed a few counter measures, like crying as soon as possible. I think that, at least with Mom, some tears seemed to telegraph that we were remorseful and had learned our lesson. But I never resented any of it. A whoopin' just came with the territory. You broke the rules, you got a whoopin'. It was essentially a contract between kids and parents with the details plainly expressed. You are not to do a certain activity or go to a certain place. If you do, you will get a whooping. End of contract. It was unwritten and certainly not signed in blood, but it *was* a contract.

Part of not resenting the whoopin', was always understanding that I deserved it. I may have occasionally argued over the degree or length of the punishment, but I always knew exactly what I had done wrong. I broke the contract. I deserved the punishment. There may have been many times that I broke a rule and did not get caught, so I didn't get a whoopin'. But those are freebies. They are not invisible marks that float above our heads, just waiting for a parent to grab one and use it against us in the event that we're actually innocent of some accused crime. They're not allowed to just say, well I'm sure you've done something today that I haven't found out about yet, so take your punishment. That's not the law. That's not the contract. All of this was true for every occasion except one. There is one time that stands out in my mind that I got a whoopin' that I did not deserve.

On the particular day of my blatant injustice, it was extremely hot. My dad was inside the house, lying on the couch with the swamp cooler pointed at him. On really hot days, he'd sometimes just lie around and listen to a baseball game on the radio. He worked extremely hard, but was smart enough to do the bulk of it in the cooler mornings and evenings.

My brother and I were outside sitting in the shade of a big tree on the edge of our yard. We'd both pulled our shirts off and soaked each other with a garden hose. We were terribly bored, and we sat there trying to think of something fun to do.

Our farm was large, covering over 2,000 acres. We had everything from trees to bicycles, and haystacks to farm animals, but on that day, nothing seemed to interest us. We thought about building a fort out of old pallets and having a rock fight. Naw. We considered finding a rope and seeing if we could run fast enough to capture a goat. Naw. It seemed that everything just felt blah that day.

It's often said that necessity is the mother of invention, and at that moment an idea popped into my bored head. By now you've already read that I had about a gazillion white chickens. There were both hens and roosters and they just loitered around our farm, lazily pecking at the ground. Most of the pretty red and black and speckled chickens were quick and difficult to catch. But the white ones, even though they could fly, were kind of dumb and slow.

I decided that it would be a great game to catch these chickens and toss them onto the roof of our little house. The idea would be to see how many chickens we could get up on the roof. My brother agreed that it would be a perfect game, and off we went in search of the white flock.

Once we got the loose herd of white chickens in our sight, we made a plan to rush at them and grab as many as we could before they realized what was happening. We ran straight at them, but they saw us coming and seemed to sense our plan and ran in every direction. Steve and I ran every which-a-way, chasing chickens into corners of the yard or corners of a pen or anywhere that we could get them hemmed up. We would grab as many as we could hold and run back towards our house. At the edge of the yard, we would pull the 4 or 5 squawking chickens from under our arms and toss them onto the roof. We'd only stop long enough to admire our work and then bound off back toward the farmyard. The whole place had an air of excitement with chickens running in every direction and the squawking cacophony could rival a first-grade band practice.

Before long, we had so many white chickens on the roof that it then became a game of attrition. We would show up with 4 chickens and throw them on the roof, but 5 might get scared and fly off. So, we realized that we had to be more precise with our throws. As we got better at the new game, we would look the roof over and find an area that didn't have a chicken and try to toss the new chicken onto the bare spot. Little by little, the brown roof started to disappear beneath the moving sea of white feathers.

I have to say that this was enormous fun and may have been the greatest game that we had ever devised. When it seemed that we had finally hit maximum capacity, we stood back with great joy and admired the roof of our little house completely covered in white chickens.

But as with any other exciting game, there is *always* going to be an adult who puts it in their mind to ruin it. I heard my dad's socked feet pounding through the house on the wooden floor, headed for the back door. As expected, the door flew open and Dad skidded to a stop, took two steps off the porch and looked up at the pure white roof.

Every one of the hundreds of white chickens were squawking as loud as they could squawk. I had a big proud grin on my face as Dad turned and yelled "What the hell are you two doing?" His colorful language got even louder and darker as he watched white chicken poop drip from the eves. He ended the tirade by pointing a big finger at us and yelling that we had exactly one minute to get every gawdamn chicken off that gawdamn roof and if he ever saw another gawdamn chicken up there he'd beat both of our gawdamn asses.

There was the contract and the terms. No more chickens on the roof, otherwise, ass-whooping. Clear as day.

We had been up on the roof many times and it was no feat for us both to shimmy up a porch post, throw a leg and pull ourselves onto the roof. As we walked across, cackling chickens flew in every direction. But I must confess, the whole place looked pretty gross. There was hardly a place to step that wasn't coated in slimy white and green chicken shit. Even from a farm boy's perspective, it wasn't pretty. But before long, every chicken had flown off and we were back to sitting in the shade beneath our tree.

So, we sat under the tree, right back where we started. Hot and bored. Dejected and dispirited. We just sat and took turns talking about Dad's overbearing rules about everything. I would never have dreamed that he'd have a fit about something as benign as a bunch of chickens on a roof. Heck, pigeons do it all the time.

Pops seemed to have no sense of fun. He seemed to have no interest at all in ensuring that his two boys had any excitement in their lives. Yes, he took us fishing, and yes, he might take us bowling once in a while. Sure, he would take us to the carnival when it was in town and once even drove us three hours to the State Fair in Sacramento. OK, he may have even taken us to Disneyland once and let us stay in a motel with a real swimming pool. He may have even occasionally got us into a big tire and rolled us down the little loading-ramp hill. But in that moment, we settled into the fact that he just didn't care about us.

As we sat there with our faces hanging, I faintly heard a throaty cluck coming from behind the tree. I knew instantly what it was, and fear fell over my whole body.

It was Satan.

Back then, I could boss around any chicken on our property. At just the clap of my hands, a hundred chickens would run for cover. Rooster or hen, they got out of my way when I walked by. But there was one chicken that I didn't mess with. It was a sinister red rooster that all of us kids called El Gallo del Diablo. The Devil Rooster!

This rooster wasn't much bigger than the white chickens. Its feathers were red and black and when it stood in the sun, it was covered in a beautiful iridescent blue and green sheen. Its barbarous head was covered in a blood-red comb and its spurs stuck out from its legs like little daggers. This chicken didn't walk. It strutted.

But it was as dangerous as it was beautiful. With no provocation, it would fly at you and flog you and stab you with its spurs. It would do everything within its formidable power to peck your eyes out. Every kid on the ranch, big, little and in between, lived in fear of this bird. Most every farm kid had suffered the humiliation of being seen crying with little bloody peck marks all over their legs and back.

And here it was, now only twenty feet from me and staring me in the eye. My mind quickly went into survival mode and ran through my options. I could roll and try to get behind the safety of the tree trunk. I could run and try to reach our front door before it dug its spurs into my bare back. Or I could just face it and try to fend it off with my bare hands. Unfortunately, all of those options were ripped away when, in less than a precious heartbeat, I realized it was in flight and coming straight for my face. I put my head down, crossed my arms over my chest, and braced for the pain.

In the next moment, I felt the wind from its wings beating over my head. The feared rooster had completely missed me. How could this be? I turned my head to see it gaining altitude and making a big, graceful turn to the left. The thankfulness of not being torn to shreds was short-lived when I realized the chicken's evil motive in flying over my head. Before I could even scream "nooooooo!" the big bird circled even higher and then headed straight for our roof. The flapping demon dropped its scaly landing gear and skidded across the roof shingles with the force and noise of a 747 landing on a gravel runway. It eventually came to a stop just above our front door.

At that point, everything got quiet. The whole barnyard seemed to sense the tension of the moment. I cocked my ear toward the house and listened. Within seconds, I again heard Dad's socked feet, bounding across the living room floor. The front door busted open, dad jumped out and turned to look up towards the roof. There was the chicken from hell, staring straight down at him. They locked eyes just long enough for the monster to ruffle its wings and let out a devilish crow.

Dad was pulling off his belt before his second step in our direction. Steve and I both pleaded and screamed that we did not do it! "The rooster flew up there on his own! Dad, I swear, I didn't do it! I swear!"

My pleading fell on deaf ears. But as dad bounded towards me, I decided to try a maneuver that I'd never tried before. RUN. I knew that running always made a whoopin' worse, but maybe I felt justified due to my innocence. Or maybe I was counting on the fact that dad was in his socks and wouldn't want to chase me. Neither thought mattered much anyway, because before I could even pick an escape direction, Pops had a hold of me. With no hesitation or words, he followed through with exactly what he said he would do if he ever saw another chicken on that roof.

The whoopin' really wasn't much by his standards. I'd had worse. But it hurt to a deeper level because I didn't deserve it. This broke the code. The chicken flew up there all by himself. It was the work of the devil. I was innocent. I had seen enough westerns on TV to know that even innocent men occasionally get hanged. But we had a contract and I had faith in the family judicial system that was now broken.

As Dad stomped back to the house with leaves and grass stuck to his socks, his folded black leather belt hanging from his hand, he yelled out to the whole farm or maybe to the whole world:

"I ought to kill that gawdamn rooster!!"

Well, at least the ruckus ended with something where he and I could finally be in perfect agreement!

OK Pops! I'll find some Holy water and you get a wooden stake. That chicken is the devil!

* * *

TIME TO THINK

12

TIME TO THINK

When I was a kid, I drove a farm tractor for my dad. It was the most boring job I ever had. I would get on a big Allis-Chalmers track layer, pulling a disc, and head to the field. I would drive across the field at about three mph, pointing the tractor toward the other end. In about ten minutes, I would reach the end of the field, pull the left-hand turning brake, spin the tractor around, and head back in the other direction. Ten minutes later, I would do the same thing again. Up and back. All day.

It was so terribly boring, that in order to help me a little, my dad would give me a thought exercise in the form of a question each morning when he dropped me off.

Dad had a few faults, like insisting twelve-year-old kids were legitimate farm labor, but he was extremely smart. He had taught himself how to read and how to do math. He grew up in rural Arkansas and only went to school through the fourth grade. My grandma told me that the last two of those years, he only went to school on picture day.

Dad was an early adopter and usually had the cool gadgets before anyone even knew what they were. He had Polaroid cameras, electric razors, an eight-track player, and a CB radio. He was probably the first person in our town to own a handheld calculator. I remember it well. It was about half the size of a shoe box lid, had + - x ÷ buttons, and if you typed 7734 and turned it upside down, it spelled hELL.

So, each morning when dad dropped me off at the tractor, he would ask me a question and I was to think about it, ponder on it, and reason through it all day. I was supposed to tell him the answer when he picked me up at the end of the ten or twelve-hour day.

Sometimes they were math questions, but always with a life lesson. One time he asked me which one is worse, to have 75% of the people mad at you 50% of the time, or to have 50% of the people mad at you 75% of the time? I tried every possible way to get a mathematical answer, but it really wasn't a mathematical question.

When I finally came up with an answer, he told me it was actually a trick question, and that the answer was neither. It is better to try to live your life so that nobody is ever mad at you.

During my career as a twelve-year-old professional tractor driver, there were many intriguing questions. Probably hundreds. But one question sticks out in my mind particularly well. In that question, he introduced me to the concept of the scientific method. He asked me if a scarecrow was an effective way to keep crows out of a garden? At the time, it seemed like a softball question for a farm kid. But it really started an eye-opening discussion that lasted for a few days.

While I stared over the long hood of the noisy tractor, I took what I knew and started thinking. We have a garden, we have a scarecrow, and I have never seen crows in our garden. I'm sure that I veered into many side questions like, how do crows fly? Why does corn have hair? Why are gardens always in a rectangle? But at the end of the day, I said yes, a scarecrow is effective at keeping crows out of a garden. I knew that answer was way too easy, and Dad would never accept it. But I went with it anyway.

After hearing my answer, Dad then started asking me about all the variables involved. "Are there even crows in the area? Is there anything in the garden that a crow would even eat? Do they even eat corn? Is there anything else in the garden that could scare them away...like people working? So maybe it's not even the scarecrow. What if we didn't have a scarecrow, would there still be no crows in the garden?"

During the next week of conversations, we talked about how we would set up some kind of experiment that would control all those variables and give us a good result.

Looking back, I know that those questions really set me up to think about bigger issues and to question statistics, data, reasoning, and the validity of other people's conclusions. I think it also steered me towards a life in science.

All of Dad's thought questions got progressively harder as I grew up. A couple of years later, he asked me a math question that really opened the door toward me thinking about college.

One day he asked me this.

"Let's say that a sixteen-year-old boy drives a tractor ten hours every day. He drives it when it's as hot as hell and he drives it when it's as cold as ice. He drives it to the end of the field, turns around and drives it back. Up and back all day. Up and back. It's boring as hell. Let's say the sixteen-year-old boy gets his girlfriend pregnant. How many days per week will he have to drive the tractor up and back all day to pay the bills for him and his girlfriend and their baby. He'll need money for rent, and he'll have to buy a bunch of furniture. He'll have to buy enough groceries to feed them all. He'll need a car and then gas and insurance. He'll have to pay for hospitals and doctor's visits. He'll need clothes for all of them. He'll have to pay for electricity to keep the lights on. Oh, I'm sure there's lots more that you can think of, since you're a sixteen-year-old boy. Just try to add all that up and see how many days per week the boy will have to work driving the boring tractor and if he'll ever get a day off. Then we can explore how much the kid would make if he didn't get his girlfriend pregnant and went to college."

I'm thankful that he spared me the embarrassment of following up the next week by asking me how girls get pregnant and how it could be avoided. He didn't have to ask. I had a pretty good idea. But he made his point, and I spent many hours re-examining my commitment as a student and a commitment that I wouldn't be a teenage father that had to drive a tractor eleven days a week just to pay the bills.

Pops knew what he was doing. Years later when I was in college and learning all kinds of new stuff, I thought about Dad's thought questions. I wondered if he had ever got past the fourth grade and managed to be on a university campus a few times, even if it was just on picture day, if he might have asked me a question like this: If an ol' boy named Schrödinger had put a cat in a box with radioactive material and a flask of poison, was the cat alive or dead?

You can Google that one (Please do! "Schrödinger's cat"), but just trust me, it's a funny as heck ending to this story.

* * *

TIME TO THINK

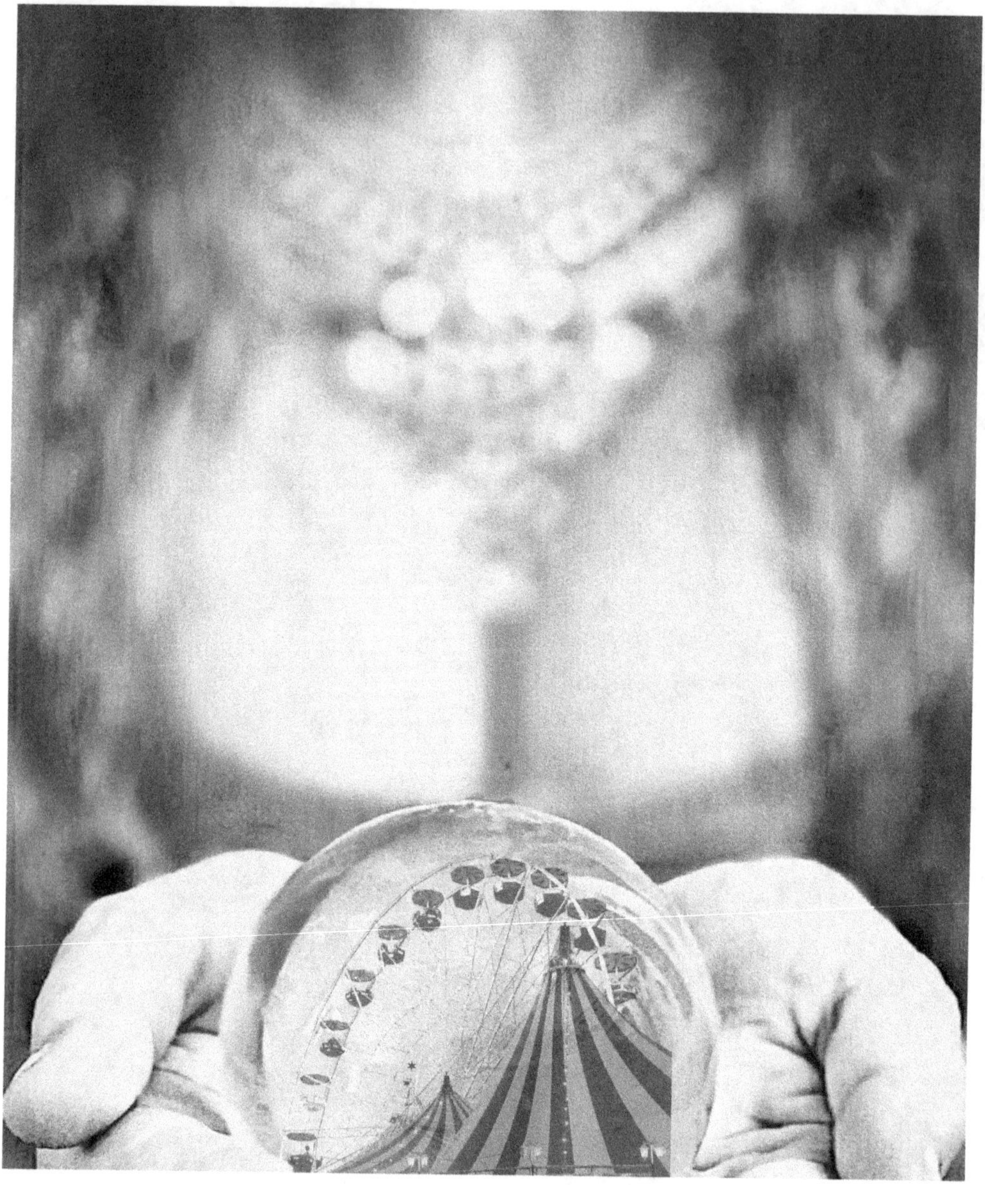

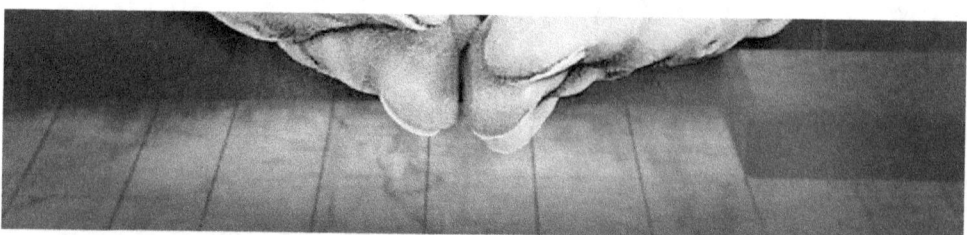

MONEY LAUNDERING

13

MONEY LAUNDERING

When I was a kid living on our farm, we were poor, but that didn't mean that I didn't have money. Even as a kid, I was enterprising, and fortunately for me, the things that interested me were also things that multiplied. Pigeons laid eggs, which made more pigeons. Chickens laid eggs, which made more chickens. Pigs had piglets, which made more pigs. So, I always had something that I could sell or barter. Yes, I'd make a dollar here and there on pigeons and chicks, but the real money came from my one foray into raising swine.

On one particularly shrewd day, I traded a bunch of chickens for a freshly weaned little piglet that turned out to be a female. I kept the little pig in a pen at a far corner of our farm. That barnyard area was a mess of little corrals, shoddy barns, and make-shift pens. Every worker on our farm and men from surrounding farms all kept their livestock there, so it was easy to hide my pig within the assortment of goats, ponies, and other farm creatures. I kept some of my chickens there, so it didn't raise any suspicion when I went there each day. Most farmers worked to keep the government out of their business. I worked to keep my parents out of mine. My Farmer Rawge side-hustle money was my own.

I quickly learned that chickens were pretty easy to keep fed, but a pig was a whole different story. Luckily, one of the crops on our farm was barley grain, and pigs loved barley. After the harvest was over, some resourceful adult would spend a Sunday running the harvester back over some of the rows that were left behind by the first harvester. In a few hours, the harvester would have gleaned what little grain was missed the first time, and we'd have a full hopper to dump at the corner of the barnyard where we kept feed. I'd soak the barley in a big barrel until it swelled and fermented, and then I'd feed it to the piglet. Between the barley and kitchen scraps that I snuck from our house, I managed to raise the little pink-nosed baby into a full-grown sow. Once the pig was grown and the time was right, a Mexican neighbor walked his boar over and left it in my pen for a couple of days. Then, just as planned, three months, three weeks, and three days later, I had twelve little baby piglets.

As much as I struggled to keep the grown pig fed, I knew it would be tough to keep all those little mouths full. So, the moment they were weaned, I put the word out that they were for sale. One piglet had to go to the guy who walked his boar the three miles to and from my pen, but I still had eleven to sell. Since I kept my parents in the dark about my illicit enterprise, I was thus at the mercy of black-market, behind-closed-doors capitalism. To wash my hands of some of the sneaking around, I took the first low-ball offer that came along. I wasn't bothered by the ultimate fate of the little pigs. I knew that they'd be fed for a few months, and then they'd be eaten. I'd sung the "This Little Piggy" nursery rhyme many times. I knew all too well that the little piggy that "went to market" wasn't going shopping, but this was no time for emotions. This was business.

I earned $40 from the quick sale, hid it in a can and buried it in my chicken pen. It was the same can that once held the $100 I won in a World Series pool, but that money was long gone. I blew through it like any other redneck who had won the lottery. Now, I had two $20 bills and was faced with the hardest part for a kid with money. I needed to launder it and get it converted into smaller and more easily spendable bills. Dollar bills could fly under my parent's radar. Twenties could not.

Everyone at the only little bank in town knew my folks, so I couldn't walk in and ask to break the pair of $20s. They'd know something was up and get word to my parents. The same was true at most any market in town. Surely, if I walked up to the counter at the grocery store and offered to pay for my 10-cent grape Nehi with a $20 bill, old Ray Kuchner would grab it and ask where I got it. So, I knew I'd just have to keep it hidden until an opportunity came along.

One of the problems of being the richest kid in the middle of nowhere is that money will burn a hole in your pocket because there's no place to spend it. But that all changed the moment I heard my dad say, "Hey Kids, on Saturday we're driving to Bakersfield to visit your granny." Well, hallelujah, my prayers were answered! Bakersfield had something I needed: The Swap-O-Rama! A side trip to that unsung 14th Greatest Show on Earth was as much a part of a visit to Granny's as her pecan pie and home-made ice cream.

True to Pop's word, we loaded up the car on Saturday and drove an hour and a half to Bakersfield. After spending the morning with Granny and Papa Myron, my brother and I, along with a bunch of relatives, rolled into the Swap-O-Rama parking lot in two packed cars. Adults had to pay a small charge, but kids got in free. Once inside, my dad gave 50 cents each to Steve and me. Since it was a rather generous amount, there were likely a few beers involved in his decision. He handed the quarters to us and said the same thing he always said. "Be back right here at 4 o'clock! DO NOT make me have to go looking for you!" I glanced at his face and knew he meant business. Come hell or high-water, I'd be standing there at 4 pm.

The Swap-O-Rama was a magnificent place, part swap-meet, part carnival, and part circus side-show. There were seemingly miles of rows with people selling their junk, but the last few rows were where the fun happened. The carnival. Steve and I headed straight there, guided by a rusty little Ferris wheel that stood above everything else.

Once safely secluded in the carnival area and out of Dad's sight, it was time to get to work and launder some piglet money. The key to laundering money is to not have to pay much for it. My plan was to find something that cost a quarter or less but with the difficult twist that the seller had to have enough change to break a $20 bill. Since we were there in the afternoon, I was hoping that the vendors were all flush with cash. But I was a little worried because the whole place was a bit empty for a weekend.

Just past the Ferris Wheel, we walked by a little trailer that had a flashy marquee painted on the side.

COME SEE THE BIGGEST RATS IN THE ENTIRE WORLD!
CAPTURED WITHIN THE DARKEST DUNGEONS OF ENGLAND!

The side of the trailer was painted with big, nasty-looking rats with glowing red eyes. But I didn't fall for it this time since we'd already been fooled once. Inside were five capybaras eating carrots on some fake grass. I told the operator that I had an encyclopedia at home and that they weren't rats, and they absolutely weren't captured in dungeons! I argued that they were more likely captured from a river in South America and insisted that I get my money back. He countered that rats and capybaras were both in the rodent family, so technically they were rats. He got loud, and since I really didn't want any trouble, I moved along. But I did tell a father and his kid who were looking it over that it was bogus and not to waste their money.

The next trailer was the side-show with **COME SEE THE FREAKS OF NATURE** painted in old-time lettering. The trailers had big paintings of a two-headed cow and a two-headed cobra with fierce fangs that were dripping with venom. Also pictured were a giant dragonfly, a colorful man-eating piranha, and, finally, a painting of a child happily riding on the back of a giant tortoise. But again, I'd already been fooled by this one. The two-headed snake and the man-eating piranha were in quart-sized jars filled with alcohol. The two-headed cow was a bad taxidermy of a calf with a second head sewn on. The dragonfly was a fossil, and the giant tortoise ride required a separate fee and even more if you wanted a Polaroid picture. I was there to launder money, but I refused to launder it with crooks.

I just kept moving along, up one side of a row, then back down on the opposite side. Fun little carnival rides and ice-cream vendors beckoned to me, but I couldn't let myself get pulled in. This wasn't the time for entertainment. I had money to launder, and I needed to do it quickly. This was business! I just needed to find something that was cheap and would provide plenty of change. Surely, I could find something for a quarter and get $19.75 back.

Steve quickly spent his quarters on ice cream and candy and then got bored with me. I was happy when he ambled off to find Mom and Dad. Perfect! Now I could make it happen. I went to vendor after vendor, but no one was able to give change for a 25-cent purchase. Although I was slowly running out of time, I refused to entertain the idea of buying something for 50 cents or a dollar just to break my bill. That thought was even more troubling when I knew I'd have to do it twice. Spending a whole dollar to get change would just be bad business!

As I frantically approached booth after booth, I happened by a trailer that I had never seen before. In big fancy lettering:

GYPSY FORTUNE TELLER AND PALM READER
SEE YOUR FUTURE!

~

MISS ZARA
THE MOST FAMED FORTUNE TELLER ON EARTH!

A man stood next to a table in front the trailer. I was about out of options and time, so I walked over and asked him what it was all about. He told me some nonsense about the beautiful and mystical Miss Zara looking at the lines in my hand and predicting my future. My desperation nudged me just enough to ask him how much this prediction would cost. He looked me in the eye and told me that the entirety of my future could be revealed for the mere sum of one thin dollar. I was shocked. With the most incredulous look that a 10-year-old could muster, I stared him back squarely in the eye and said, "What!?!? A whole dollar just for some stupid information!?!? No way!" Yet, the very moment I turned to walk away in disgust, the beautiful and exotic Miss Zara, the very woman the gentleman had mentioned, appeared almost out of nowhere and sat down in the chair in front of me.

In less than a half second, my contempt for the idea changed completely. Maybe I could have been won over by her hair, as shiny and black as a raven's feathers, but in that moment, all I saw was a deeply scooped billowy blouse overflowing with bosoms. I snapped around to the gentleman and asked if he had change for a twenty. He nodded yes. I asked if he had the change in ones. He replied that he just happened to be in possession of a large number of ones and would happily part with some of them. He counted out nineteen and looked me in the eye. I handed him my $20 bill with one hand as I grabbed the stack of $1 bills with the other. I stuck the wad in my pocket, sat down in the chair, and turned my complete attention to the buxom fortune teller.

Miss Zara picked up my hand and traced the lines of my palm with her soft fingers. The whole while as she talked in a sensuous voice, telling me about each line, my eyes remained fixed on her breasts. They seemed as smooth as any skin I'd ever seen. As she talked and stroked my palm, she would occasionally stand up and bend in toward me to get a better feel for my life. Each time she bent over, her loose blouse would fall away and for a few moments, everything beneath could be seen. I had never seen bare breasts before outside of a magazine, so all I could do was stare. And stare. And stare. And then it was over. Miss Zara released my hand and thanked me.

Again, I was shocked. No! I wasn't ready to be done! I quickly asked her about my other hand. Maybe it had something even more profound to tell. Maybe my true future was held in that palm? Without taking my eyes off of the beautiful Zara, I snapped the other $20 bill out of my pocket and aimed it toward the man with the $1 bills. He took it, handed me back my change, and the exotic process of conjecturing my future began again.

Apparently, my left hand required Miss Zara to stand up even more. For this important work, she would lean in further, shake her shoulders, and trace the faint lines past my palm and well up my arm. Again, she spoke the whole while in her thin and sensuous voice. And again, I just stared. I was transfixed on what was before my eyes and oblivious to everything else around me. Time slowed, and the whole world just melted away.

But even in my beguiled state, I suddenly seemed to faintly hear my name, which gradually became louder. Soon it was loud enough that I snapped out of my haze and saw my brother yelling at me from the roped-off entry. "Dad is looking for you!" Oh, crap! I'd lost track of time. I yanked my arm and jumped to my feet, sticking my hand in my pocket to push down the stack of money and everything else that was trying to bulge out. I turned and, without a word, ran for the gate. In just a few minutes, I was out of breath and getting a full verbal ripping from my dad for not being at the parking lot when I was told to be.

In the back of the station wagon on the way home, Steve asked, "Who was that woman?" I told him to shut up, that it was just business. I didn't tell him that I was glad he showed up when he did, or I'd have probably gotten Miss Zara to read the lines on my forehead, the wrinkles on my knees, and anything else I could find until I was out of dollars.

But here is the remarkable part of this story. I had both palms read by Miss Zara, arguably the most famed psychic in all the land. The exotic and beautiful fortune teller had spoken for over half an hour about my future. And now, fifty years have passed since that day. This is the greatest opportunity in the history of fortune telling to test the validity of the whole crystal-gazing and palm-reading arts! Was any of it true? How much of it actually came to pass?

So, in my precious time with Miss Zara, this is what I can recall:

Titties. That's it. Zero words. Just titties.

I could describe to you exactly what they looked like, their shape, their color, how they moved, and most anything else about them. But I can't tell you a single word that passed through Miss Zara's lips. I'm sorry. A rare opportunity was missed. I could have written volumes of scientific literature with my empirical observations. But no, I've let the world down.

However, one of the event's predictions has been repeatedly verified during my subsequent fifty-year history. Men may be all business until a revealing silk dress, a big pair of bosoms, and a soft voice enters the picture. And then... well...that might be the recipe to relieve them of their $1 bills and a good portion of their common sense.

* * *

LOVE FOR FAMILY

14

LOVE FOR FAMILY

A big thing happened in 1976. I got a driver's license. But even more exciting, my dad bought me a black 1970 El Camino with fat mag wheels and an engine too big for a 16-year-old boy. Everyone else my age had a license, but very few had a car, so I was often a taxi. But back then if you had a truck bed, you were also occasionally a bus.

On one summer evening after work, I cleaned up and was planning to drive into Coalinga, 20 miles away. I was in the front yard waiting for my friend Eddie to get dropped off. He lived a couple of ranches away. On our way to town, we would stop by the 5-Mile Cotton Gin and pick up our friend Montie. We'd all spend the evening in town, hanging out with friends and talking to girls. We needed to look our best, and I reeked of Musk cologne.

A little after 5 pm, a station wagon rolled up on the dirt road and Eddie hopped out. He was walking slowly, but before he even got close, I could tell that something was wrong. Something was seriously wrong, and it was wrong with his head. At first, I thought that maybe he'd been in an accident, but his head wasn't bloody or anything like that. It was just disfigured.

"Damn Eddie, you look like you've been shot at and missed, but shit at and hit! What the hell happened to your head?" I asked.

"Oh, man. It's my little sister. Uh...she's trying to get into beauty college school."

"So what? You let her practice on you?"

"Yeah, she needs the practice."

"Shit, yeah, she needs the practice! Damn, Eddie!"

I looked it over, grabbing his shoulders and turning him to the side for a better look. Eddie always had a pretty nice shock of hair. But this was bad. It's hard to describe, but it was like she took a whole lot off of one side but then forgot the other side. The shaved line on the back of his neck was way too high and whatever she had done, the front just fell to the wrong direction.

"Guess she styled it, too?"

"Yep, she used a brush and a blow dryer thing," Eddie said, sheepishly.

"Damn! OK. Let me think a minute. Hey, if we hurry, we can run into Huron to Ray's Barber Shop, and maybe he can fix it. I've got $5."

"Oh man. Naw. That might hurt her feelings. I'll just wait. It'll grow out."

And it did grow out. A couple of months later, you could hardly tell what had happened. Throughout the whole summer though, Eddie had to explain to folks what happened, over and over. By the time school started, his hair had grown back, and his sister had gotten better at cutting and styling and had evened it up a bit.

It took a while for me to realize how that episode affected me. Hardly a day didn't go by that I wasn't angry with my sisters or brother for something they did or the way they acted. But Eddie's haircut would convict me, and my anger would float out of my mind. It would be replaced by a picture of Eddie's little sister. I could see her standing with a brush and scissors in her hand, staring at lopsided Eddie sitting in a chair with a towel draped over his shoulders. Both of them always had a loving smile on their faces. Shortly after that memory, I'd have a smile, too.

* * *

LOVE FOR FAMILY

FISHAHOLIC

15

FISHAHOLIC

I've always loved to fish. When I was a kid, there wasn't much that I'd rather do and I begged my dad to take me fishing every weekend. Later, when I had a car and a driver's license, I got serious about it. Probably too serious. This is a fun parody about that time.

"Hi, my name is Roger Jones and... and I'm a fishaholic." I could hardly say the words as I stood in a room with ten or fifteen other fishaholics. Instantly there were cheers and applause, letting me know I wasn't alone. I shivered as I gazed across the room at the faces of the others and saw how the years of fishing had taken their toll. I could see the bony arthritis in their elbows from casting for hours on end. I could see their eyes were frozen into a permanent squint from forever scanning the water surface in hopes of locating the ripples of a feeding fish. These men were mere shells of their former selves and I had seen enough. I was ready to quit.

Yes, I am a fishaholic. I am a fishaholic and I want help. The words came a little easier after I had seen what I might soon turn into. With my new comrades around me, I turned to face the crowd. It was time to tell my story.

It all started when I was about ten or twelve years old. That's when I started hanging out with the guys. If peer pressure could be measured with a tire pressure gauge, I probably had about 500 pounds per square inch. Yes, that old gang had quite an influence on me. One of the older kids asked me to sneak out of the house one night and go fishing with them. I tried to tell them that my mother took a dim view of fishing and that she forbade even my father to fish. However, he did slip around and do it a bit behind her back. The older boys all got a real good laugh at my attempt to do the right thing. They only had to call me a sissy about three times before this mama's boy gave in.

That Friday night it was all arranged, at midnight I would sneak out of my bedroom window. I met the gang at the secret spot down on the river. One of the older boys brought me an old fishing pole that he had borrowed from his dad. I used the term borrowed here very loosely because I doubt he went to the trouble to ask. We fished that night for hours and it felt so good. The whole while we swapped stories about hunting-dogs and pocket-knives and all of the other finer things in 10-year-old lives.

We fished that night until the first purple hints of a sun appeared in the eastern sky. One by one, the guys started shuffling their weary feet toward home to be back in bed before their families woke up. I knew that the discovery of an open window and my empty bed might prove fatal for me, so I double-timed it the whole way home. I was ready to get back through my window and sleep my Saturday away.

I can still remember those horrible words I heard a few mere seconds after I snuck my near-lifeless body into bed. "Knock! Knock! Get up boy and come down to breakfast. I want you to help me around the farm today."

Dad worked me hard for about ten hours. By the end of that day, I felt like I was near death. My mom told me that I looked terrible. She thought I was coming down with something and made me drink a big dose of cod liver oil. It was the most foul-tasting panacea on earth, but the good news was she sent me to bed.

Laying there that evening I went over the events of the previous night. I caught my first fish and got my first taste of fishing. It all seemed so innocent. Little did I know that the nightmare had begun.

Soon I found myself slipping around and trying to fish more and more. I would sneak around from pond to pond, and word quickly spread around the old ladies' gossip circles that the oldest Jones boy fished when his parents weren't looking. My mom would catch me coming home late from school and head me off at the door. "Where have *you* been?" she would ask with a raised eyebrow. "You should have been home hours ago! Have you been out fishing? Let me smell your hands!"

Fishy smelling hands could give you away in a heartbeat. I was very thankful for lemon scented hand soap. I would tell Mom not to worry, I would never go fishing, not even when I grew up. As she walked away, I would pull my hand from my back and then uncross my fingers. I'm sure that my mom often wondered why her son always smelled like a migrant lemon picker.

As the number of my years grew, so did my obsession with fishing. When I got old enough to fish in public, my parents met my habit with terrible dismay. My father would tell me, "Son, fishing and running around with women will get you nothing but trouble." But I was 21 years old and dang-sure didn't need a couple of old folks telling me how to run my life.

After my first six or seven years of junior college, I got married. My wife was a nice country girl and quite understanding. She knew that I fished a little, but only for social reasons. She never pitched a fit on the few nights a week that I'd go out and cast a few with the boys. I might come home late, smelling a little fishy, but she never made a scene.

But, like any farm boy knows, if you're given enough rope, you'll hang yourself. One night it finally happened. I stayed out all night! A few of us were out fishing and the next thing I knew, it was morning. I raced home to find my wife in a state of total panic. "Where have you been? Why didn't you call? I've been worried sick!" She yelled in a voice that only a half-crazed hysterical woman could use. "I've called all the bait shops, and no one has seen you. Look at yourself! You're still half-fished!"

I tried to think of the right words to say, those perfect words that would make everything alright again. With a dumb look on my face, I searched my mind for the perfect words that a woman would want to hear but all that came out was, "Honey, will you help me clean all these catfish?" Apparently, those weren't the right words because she stomped off and locked herself in the bedroom.

That incident was the jarring beginning of my descent into addiction. I started to fish more and more each week and sometimes all weekend. My marriage was beginning to suffer. My life was becoming a wreck. I couldn't go an entire day without fishing. I was on my way down.

I knew I was hitting bottom when I started fishing on the job. Things got so bad that I couldn't make it through an 8-hour day without fishing. While at work, if I saw a place to fish, I'd pull over and make a few casts just to get rid of the shakes. The bottom of the barrel was wrapping around me.

Before the end of that year, my wife had kicked me out and I was living in the camper shell on my truck. My parents couldn't even look me in the eye. I'd lost every friend except the handful of other addicts that I stumbled around with.

One day I was checking-out at the counter of a big bait-and-tackle store. Beside the register, I saw a small leaflet that had the words: *GOT A PROBLEM? WE CAN HELP!* My arms were full of a six-pack of night-crawlers, but I grabbed a brochure and quietly stuck it in my pocket. That evening, I pulled it out and silently read the words. *You can quit! Our program is guaranteed. Only ten days and a couple of two-day follow-ups.*

I looked around at the lonely inside of my empty camper. I made the decision—it was time to quit. I drove to the facility and walked through the door, ready to admit, "I am a fishaholic!"

Those ten days were hell. It was ten days of never catching a fish, yet I was forced to watch Jimmy Houston Outdoors until I was sick. I was forced to eat three meals a day of fish that were not freshly caught. I gagged through eating fish that had actually been purchased frozen from a store! We talked about triggers and buddy systems and sponsors. We talked about steps and serenity prayers. I walked by rooms where grown men lay crying in their beds as they watched the sun rise over the beautiful pond just outside their windows.

I have to admit, there were times that I didn't think I would make it. But on day ten, I graduated with honors. I stood with the other dozen men, all dressed in slacks. Many of us had not been without a sleeveless t-shirt and a fishing vest in twenty years. We each took our diploma, shook the director's hand, and walked out to face the world.

Yes, there are times when my arm still twitches in cast-like spasms when I pass a bait and tackle shop. There are other times when I hear voices as I walk past the rod and reel section at the department store. I still fight the steering wheel not to just cruise by the lake for a quick look.

But as they say at the FA meetings: one day at a time.

* * *

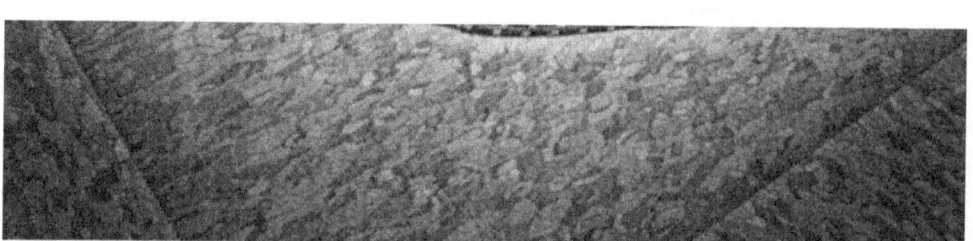

CLIMBING THE LADDER

16

CLIMBING THE LADDER

Two men were trying to climb up some very arduous steps. Each step was steep and difficult to reach. One man piled money high enough that he could easily reach the next step. The other man piled shopping carts, uniforms and grocery bags to help him reach the next step.

To continue up, the first man again used his money. He made a pile of it so high that he could easily walk to the next higher step. The other man used hard hats, gloves and work boots to stand on. He piled up his tools and climbed up the step.

This continued for some time, with one man walking on money and the other standing on the tools of his trade to reach the next step.

Somewhere up the ladder, both men found themselves on the same step. The hardworking man stopped to catch his breath. He wiped his forehead and looked back at all of his accomplishments and how far he had come. He was tired, but he smiled and was happy. The other man didn't look back at his accomplishments. He only looked up toward all that he hadn't reached and everything that he didn't have. He had a sad look on his face and wasn't happy.

One of these men was rich.

* * *

BEGINNING COMPUTER 101
MAY 4 1986

MY LIST OF RULES TO LIVE BY
1. █
2.
3.
4.
5.
6.
7.
8.
9.
10.
11.
12.

RAWGE'S RULES TO LIVE BY

17

RAWGE'S RULES TO LIVE BY

In the early 1980s, when we were all hearing about computers, I was fortunate enough to buy one. It was an IBM PC XT and I knew zero about it. It had 10 megabytes of storage and 128kb of RAM. This story isn't about PCs, but just for fun, that first big ol' PC with the little green CRT monitor could process about 330,000 "requests" per second. The smart phone that I'm writing this on can process over one trillion requests per second. We've come a long way.

Way back then, I struggled to learn about everything from DOS to spreadsheets. Everything was new. I had a word processor to write with, spreadsheets to calculate numbers and graphics programs to draw things. We were decades away from being able to grab our phone and order a copy of DOS for Dummies and have it delivered to our door before the end of the day, so I struggled.

When I was finally able to take a computer class, one of the first assignments was to type a numbered list of twelve things, format it, left-justify it, etc. I don't remember the whole assignment, but I do remember the list that I created. For that assignment, I wrote *My List of Rules to Live By*. In fact, I still have the file on a floppy disc that is so obsolete, nothing is now able to read it.

Since way back then, computers have changed drastically, but my list hasn't changed much. It has evolved, been updated, and been refined a bit, but the core is still the same.

The items on the list are intended for me, but there might be something in there that you could incorporate into your own list.

RAWGE'S 12 RULES TO LIVE BY V.20.22

1. Whatever you're doing, if you're not laughing, then you're probably not doing it right.
2. If you've got something that you don't need, before you try to sell it, search yourself hard to see if there's any way possible that you're able to give it away to someone for free.
3. Don't do anything standing up that you could possibly do while sitting down, or even better, laying down.
4. Never say "I would never." Instead, simply say "Maybe someday, but not today."
5. Never hesitate to apologize.
6. Never go to sleep without looking back at your day and planning how you will do better tomorrow.
7. Wash your face with cool water every morning and see as many sunrises as possible.
8. Live your own romance novel.
9. There are not many traits in the world that are more valuable than being a good listener.
10. More often than not, the best thing to do is to keep your mouth shut.
11. Almost nothing stays the same or lasts a lifetime. Including our troubles.
12. Love people without asking a bunch of questions first.

* * *

FACTS STRANGER THAN FICTION

18

FACTS STRANGER THAN FICTION

When I was a kid on our farm, I loved to track animals. We walked a dirt road out to the highway to catch the bus. During much of the year, the dirt at the end would be pulverized into a powder and it was perfect for absorbing tracks. I stashed a big piece of burlap in a culvert at the end of the road. Each day I would pull it out and drag it around the dirt road until it was perfectly smooth. The next day I would check out all the tracks and try to determine what took place. I'd find pheasants walking by, coyotes, rabbits, doves, and other little birds. Occasionally I'd see the tiny line of little tracks from a big fat stink bug. But I really liked the larger tracks.

I'd look at it all and try to decide what the animal was doing. Was it walking or running, lounging, or feeding. Did it ever sit... Or jump? That time each day was always fun, thought-provoking, and educational.

One day I was especially excited to get off the bus. It had rained slightly the night before and I knew that tracks would be crisp and easy to see. I walked slowly, checking my big dirt canvas and was surprised to find something odd. There was a set of human tracks coming from the dirt road and walking up to the eastbound direction of the little paved road. A grown person's tracks weren't out of place, but this pair was something I'd never seen. This odd set had a work boot on one foot and the other foot was bare. I must admit that I was stumped. A grown man had walked up our dirt road to the highway, wearing only one boot.

So, I back-tracked as best I could. I tracked it past our place and on the road headed to several of the other ranches. A few times I determined the person was running. He'd walk a bit then run. I was sure he was tiring himself out just trying to get to the highway.

Of course, I pondered this over the coming days and weeks and no explanation seemed to make sense. I never told anyone about it and eventually forgot about it.

Twenty years later, I was grown and had moved away to college. During a break, I had returned home to the ranch for a visit. It was cotton picking season and everyone worked until late at night. Cotton picking was a busy time. The mechanical pickers would start each morning as soon as the dew dried from the open cotton bolls. Dew was the enemy. The slightest moisture would cause the picking mechanisms to jam-up with cotton. The mess was difficult to clean and could even start a fire within the machine. So, in the evenings, picking halted the very moment that my dad sensed even a hint of dew on the plants. Sometimes this happens at midnight and sometimes it happens earlier. The crew never knew how long the workday would last.

One afternoon, I was standing with my dad and some workers at the end of the field. We were next to the big trailers where the cotton pickers dumped each time they returned from their round. As we were standing around, a couple of the old guys were talking about the days gone by. One of them said, "Man! You remember that time it started to rain so we all quit at five and went home way early?"

The other said, "Oh yea! Fernando went home early and surprised his wife with a Sancho! The poor old boy tried to grab his clothes and busted out through the window. He didn't get nothin' but pants, a shirt and one boot!"

I learned that the sneaky lover had to run all the way to the highway in the dark, wearing just one boot. The old timers went on to say how Fernando carried the boot around for weeks, looking to see who might have new boots and would fit into the old worn boot left behind in the fracas. It was kind of a Cinderella story, just not pretty and romantic.

But the decades-old mystery had been solved. Even the strangest things can eventually make sense. But it can take years. Maybe lots of years. I'm getting old. So, from here on out, I'm pretty much going to just sit back and say it's been long enough! Let the answers to *all* my life's mysteries start rolling in!

(*Note: Names have been changed to protect the innocent.)

* * *

THE DANGERS OF SCISSORS

19

THE DANGERS OF SCISSORS

I am sure that you have heard about the danger of scissors. You have been told not to run with them, to be careful around your fingers, and not to carry them in your pocket. I have recently learned that scissors can be far more dangerous when used by the wrong hands.

A while back, I was cutting a pattern on card stock paper to use as a guide while doing some metal work. I was almost finished cutting around the drawn lines when I heard a "snap" and I found myself holding two pieces of scissors. No problem, I thought. I quickly located a small bolt, placed it into the hole that previously held a rivet and resumed my cutting. Apparently, a small bolt and nut cannot replace a three-cent rivet, as the pair would no longer cut. The blades still went up and down and made some scissor-like noises but produced no cutting action. Oh well, the house is full of scissors.

I turned to my eight-year-old son and sent him to the house to fetch a pair from our "junk" drawer. He returned, holding a pretty pair of shiny, blue-handled scissors. I took them from his hand and started cutting. Wow!! This was nothing like the worn-out pair of scissors we had in our toolbox. This was a *REAL* pair of scissors. They cut so smoothly, and each edge of the pattern material looked like it had been cut at a factory. The blades sliced through the heavy material with ease and followed even the trickiest curves. It was so much fun, we finished making the original pattern and then went ahead and made a bunch of new fancy patterns for everything we planned to cut for the next year!

About two days later, I was laying on the concrete driveway looking up at the bottom of a truck, when my beautiful wife came out to see if I was making an oily mess. She hadn't even fully stopped her walk when she noticed the greasy pair of scissors buried three wrenches deep in my toolbox.

"Are those my good sewing scissors?" she screamed in a voice so high and mean that the hair on the back of my neck stood to attention. As with previous encounters with this voice, I was overcome with fear. I tried to speak, but only managed to look toward the toolbox with my mouth hanging open.

"Yes! Those scissors!!!!" she screamed. Her eyes had narrowed into slits and her eyebrows had slanted into the deep "V" typically reserved for cartoon villains. She was the perfect picture of a woman about to kill her husband.

"How did they get out here??!!" she shrieked.

After a few seconds, I regained some of my strength. My mind raced as I searched for an explanation that could keep me alive. The only thing I could think of was to throw the boy under the bus.

"Are those yours, baby?" I asked in my *take my wallet, my money, but please don't kill me* voice.

"The boy brought them out here. I had no idea where he got 'em!"

She reached in and picked up the greasy scissors with her finger and thumb, the way someone might pick up a dead mouse by its tail. She glared at me one last time and disappeared around the corner, holding the nasty scissors at arm's length.

"These scissors cost me $150! If you've torn them up, I'll beat your ....!" and the front door slammed behind her.

I guess the scissors cleaned up ok and still cut her muslin and percale fabrics. I'm sure they're tucked safely back into her cute little wicker sewing basket. Sadly, I'm now back to gnawing cardboard patterns with my crude black and silver shop scissors. But I will never forget the magical afternoon I spent with the sewing scissors. Sometimes, when I am alone in the shop, I close my eyes and find my mind cutting graceful curves through a piece of pattern material, like a downhill skier cutting slaloms on a beautiful powdery mountain.

THE DANGERS OF SCISSORS

TRUST

20

TRUST

Everyone should be trusted, at least a little, until they give you reason to distrust them. That's the way it should be. But I must confess, there are some groups of people that I typically just do not trust. I know it's not fair, but they start out towards the bottom of the trustworthy list. It doesn't mean that none of them can be trusted, it's just that they start at the bottom and then have to work their way up. Here's my list.

1. T.V. Preachers
2. Politicians
3. Rich people
4. Men that don't carry a pocketknife
5. Fisherman
6. Teen-aged boys
7. Skinny cooks
8. Any phone caller that starts off with "Hello Mr. Jones."
9. Mechanics without at least a little gray hair
10. Court-appointed lawyers

* * *

A HEART'S DESIRE

21

A HEART'S DESIRE

During the summer of 1998, I took a few weeks to drive around and see some of our beautiful mountain states. It was a solo trip, with just me and Doc, my red heeler cattle dog. I didn't have a real agenda or itinerary, so I just headed east from Sacramento. I had a few state maps that I had gotten from AAA and a big atlas as my guide. Ultimately, I was headed to Yellowstone and to see the elk antler sculptures in Jackson Hole Wyoming. But I was in no hurry.

During most days, I drove east a few hours and then found something on the map that sounded interesting. I'd veer off the highway and spend the day exploring around a lake, a hot spring or most any other natural feature that caught my attention.

On the second day, I drove 22 miles off the highway to camp at a small lake in Utah. About 20 miles up the road, I passed by a big wide spot with about 50-feet of cliff face jutting up on one side and a beautiful small valley on the other side. I continued up the road and just a bit farther, I found the lake and small campground. There was not a soul around. The gate was guarded by an *iron ranger*, a place to pay your camping fee even if there was no attendant there to take your money. The contraption relied on the honor system, although it was well known that if an actual ranger showed up and you had not paid, you'd get a hefty ticket. I filled out the form with the tiny pencil and dropped in my two dollars.

I drove to the end of the road and backed my truck in between some big boulders used to separate the camping spots. There, if someone else did show up, I'd still have some privacy. I got out and stretched my legs while Doc visited every tree and rock in the area. We walked around the little lake shore, and I skipped a few flat rocks on the water.

Towards early evening, I cooked some noodles on my little camp stove and drank a Coke from my ice chest. I decided to take my guitar and walk back towards the little cliff I had seen above the road. It was a perfect evening for me to play a concert for all the birds, butterflies, and trees.

It was just a short walk and soon I was sitting on a rock looking down at the little road about 50 feet below. Doc found a comfortable spot in the shade and laid down. I pulled my guitar off my back, tuned it a bit, and strummed a few chords. I heard a faint train whistle way off in the distance, so I started singing.

"Riding on the city of New Orleans.... Illinois Central ... Monday morning mail... Fifteen cars and fifteen restless riders... Three conductors and 25 sacks of mail...."

I'm sure that the birds and the bugs and the lizards thought it was the greatest voice and song that they'd ever heard!

But before I even got to the first chorus, I heard the hint of a low rumble sound. I stopped playing and looked hard towards the highway. I could see dust from a car coming up the road. I shook my head at the thought of another visitor here to break up my peace and solitude. I watched the dust as it got closer and closer. When it finally rounded the nearest curve, I could see that it wasn't a car. It was a bus – an old school bus that had been painted green and had writing on the side.

When it got below me, it pulled over onto the big wide area on the road. Before the dust even settled, people started piling out. They were all a little younger than me and dressed in boho skirts, shorts, and sandals. They pulled out a couple of tables and a few chairs and started setting up for a meal. As they scurried around, I wondered why they didn't drive another mile up to the campground. But judging from the rattly bus, I thought that maybe they didn't want to pay the two dollars to get in.

As they busied around, I knew it was just a matter of time until someone looked up and said, hey, there's a guy up there with a guitar and then they'd demand that I play them a song!

There I was, up on a stone stage with an audience scattered below me. That might have been as close as I'd ever get to a Red Rock moment! My mind raced through my repertoire of songs. What should I play? How about a solid Woody Guthrie song like *This Land is Your Land, This Land is My Land*? Oh, wait. I've got it! Surely out here in the middle of the mountains, those folks would love to hear *Rocky Mountain High*! Or maybe that bunch of hippie chicks would really get into my version of *Bobby McGee*.

Well, let me tell you what I played. Nothing. That's what I played. Nothing. I chickened out. I love guitar and I love singing. But I just couldn't do either in front of people. So, I stood up and quietly snuck my way back to my little two-dollar spot on the lake. I sat on the tailgate of my truck for the rest of the evening and played and sang for the grand audience of me and Doc. As the sky filled up with stars, I crawled into my sleeping bag and fell asleep, thinking of all the songs that I should have played for the hippie bus.

A few days later, I was in the Idaho mountains, camped alongside another beautiful lake. I had carefully chosen the spot, so that in the morning, I could watch the sun rise up over the Sawtooth Mountains and reflect in the glass-like water of the serene lake. I had imagined such a site, and even seen such beautiful imagery in magazines, but this was my opportunity to witness such breathtaking beauty with my own eyes.

The next morning, I got up in the dark and brewed some coffee. I grabbed my steaming cup and hiked over to a huge granite rock that I had picked out the evening before. It would be the perfect spot. I sat on the big boulder with Doc curled at my feet. I watched the eastern sky with anticipation and awe.

Well sure enough the sky turned pink, and then slowly turned to magenta and finally the fiery red of the sun started showing just above the beautiful skyline crags. At that very second, right in the middle of my once-in-a-lifetime spiritual moment, it popped in my head – why didn't you play a song for the hippies in the green bus? You coward!

The moment was ruined. Why would such a thought crowd my mind? I didn't understand it, but I guess something buried deep down in my heart's desire really wanted to perform some music for people.

About fifteen years later, a few months after my 50th birthday, I spent a couple of weeks bumming around Mississippi. I had wanted to visit the state ever since I was a kid, when Mississippi was the longest word that I could spell. The state was also one of the few that wrote back to me, when in 4th grade, I sent letters to their visitors' bureaus asking for information. I received a package from them that contained a little flag, a colorful brochure and letter saying that they'd love to have me visit someday. They played the long game and here I was, 40 years later, ready to taste their food and music and leave some tourist dollars scattered around the beautiful state.

I had prowled around the Delta for a few days, stayed the night in a converted cotton gin in Clarksdale, and visited the famed crossroads where the blues legend Robert Johnson had allegedly made a deal with the devil.

Later in the trip, I stayed for a week in a shack at a place called Tallahatchie Flats outside of Money Mississippi. The owner had assembled a collection of share-cropper shacks, outfitted them with air-conditioning units and TVs and rented them as motel units. It was a cool place on the banks of the Tallahatchie River.

Each time I made the short drive into Greenville for lunch or dinner, I'd see a little square building in the corner of a cotton field, with WABG Radio on the side in big letters. It looked like the perfect place where a few ramblers could go inside and get paid $5 for singing into a can.

One day on the way back to my shack, I saw a truck parked in the gravel parking lot beside the little building, so I went up to the door and knocked. I was greeted with a handshake from Mr. Poe, the manager of the station. He invited me in and told me all about the station and its history with Blues Music. As we talked, he would cut over and introduce the next record. He asked me if I would be willing to do a live interview about my trip through the Delta. Of course, I jumped at the chance. During the interview, Mr Poe asked all about my trip, what I do for a living, what all I've seen in Mississippi, and stuff like that. I told him about my love for music. I told him about my Reborn Guitars shop and how I've sent free guitars all over the USA and the world. He asked me about guitars and songs and other musical things. Then it happened. He asked me to get my guitar and play a song ON THE RADIO! I tried to say no and impress on him that I was way too scared and shy for something like that, but he insisted. I told him how I love guitar and music, but that it was something I did for myself and that I just didn't do it in front of anyone.

Even as I shook my head no, something crept up from deep down inside me and whispered in my ear, "You ain't getting any younger!" It may have even rolled around my mind that at some point I'd likely be watching a sensational sunrise somewhere on the Delta and I didn't want the moment ruined by another regret. Why didn't you play a song on the radio? You coward!

So, in a moment of boldness (or weakness or insanity), I ran out to my car and grabbed the $50 piece-of-junk guitar I had bought a couple days earlier at a pawn shop. Between the slamming of the car door and the few steps up to the radio station, I'd decided I'd sing *I'll Fly Away*. I could do a cool flat-pickin' intro and a lively riff in the middle. Perfect. I hustled back in, sat down, and with no practice or warm up, I was playing and singing (actually murmuring) one of my favorite guitar songs.

I can say with no hesitation, it was the worst that I have ever played or sang. I was so nervous my leg was bouncing up and down and my throat felt like someone had a grip around it. But I muddled through it. Verse. Chorus. Verse. Chorus. Done. No flat-pickin' intro. No frills. No bluegrass riffs between verses. Nothing. Just words and a buzzy chord here and there.

When I finished, Mr. Poe was a consummate professional. He helped me laugh through it with jokes about nerves and other performance killers. He told me how many times that he'd seen others who had gotten nervous and didn't give their best performance. We laughed a bit more, shook hands, and Mr. Poe said goodbye with a big smile, "I hope to see you again sometime."

About an hour later, I was sitting in my little share-cropper shack, still a little shaky from the experience, when I got a knock on my door. Of course, I didn't know a soul in the area, so it was a bit of a surprise. I answered the door and the guy standing there said, "Hey man, we heard you on the radio a whall-a-go. We got a bunch of musicians over in the other shack. C'mon over and hang out with us."

I went over and met about a half dozen musicians and we all had a pretty good laugh at my shaky live and impromptu performance. But there was no judgment. No criticism. No embarrassment. Just a cool bunch of guys that made me feel comfortable. I sat out all evening on their porch and listened to them talk about all their music and lives. Sid, the group's vocalist and leader, let me try out his little Martin guitar and talked to me about my guitar shop. One of the guys made a run into town and came back with a barrel full of genuine homemade Mississippi hot tamales. We had a nice evening playing music, eating hot tamales, and talking about the south.

A week later, on my red-eye flight home, I sat with my eyes closed and thought about my fears and phobias. I hadn't exactly conquered one of them, but I had shown myself that performing music was at least possible if you've got supportive people around. I vowed to myself that when I got home, I would play music. And I would do it in front of people.

Within a month of being home, I was playing rhythm guitar with Rhonda at our little forty-person church. Just like the others that I had met on my trip, Rhonda showed patience and helped me feel comfortable. Rhonda had been leading the Sunday music there for several months, but I had insisted that I'd never be seen on stage. I was a novice, but Rhonda printed special chord sheets that made everything much easier for me. She helped me through my difficulties and found little places for me to play something special when I was able. Soon, it started to feel more comfortable and enjoyable. I was always nervous during the opening song, but Rhonda would choose a first song that required little of me. That gave me some time to get past my nerves. Always, by the second song, I'd be relaxed and into the groove.

Within a year, I had formed a band called the Roots Gospel Jam. Within another year, we were playing monthly concerts to packed churches, community centers and most any place that would have us. During the next few years, we played and sang to thousands of happy folks.

Looking back through those years of self-discovery, I realized that playing and performing music was buried and hidden somewhere down in my heart's desire. I wonder what other wonderful things might be just waiting to be brought out by the right people.

Since then, I've striven to pay it forward. I've tried to be as gracious and encouraging as Mr. Poe and Sid and the other musicians that I met in Mississippi. I've tried to be as patient as Rhonda was when I play the wrong chord or sang a flat note. I'll continue trying to pass along a happy pat on the back each time I'm with someone who's trying out something new, whatever it is. I'll always try to be there and be quick to say "You tried it. You did it. You'll do even better next time. Keep on."

For every hidden pearl within our heart's desire, there's someone out there to help us crack it open and let it gleam for the world.

I hope I can be that person!

* * *

FEARS

22

FEARS

There are only a few things in this world that I'm afraid of. I'm afraid of bears and rattlesnakes and crowds. I'm also afraid of the dark. I can avoid bears and rattlesnakes. I can mostly avoid crowds. But staying out of the dark is a little more challenging.

I can't explain to you why I'm afraid of the dark. I don't believe in ghosts or spirits or vampires or monsters...in the daylight. Apparently at night I'm a little more open-minded about the possibilities.

As a result of my fear, I have a collection of flashlights. In fact, I have the best flashlights that money can buy. If a new one comes onto the market, I get it. If another new one becomes available, I've got that one too. My flashlights are the peak of technology. Most militaries would be jealous of my flashlight collection.

When I do need to venture into the dark, I get myself equipped. *Flashlight? Check. Backup flashlight?* Check. *Backup batteries?* Check. If I'm going into our attic, add a lantern and headlight to that list.

The other day I was reading some poetry and stumbled onto a line that made the hair on the back of my neck stand up. The poet had written... *And darkness fell like a curtain!*

My mind freaked out a little. What? No way! That can't happen, right? Darkness comes on at a known pace. It's predictable. The sun sets and then it slowly gets dark. I know it's coming, and I can get myself to some light. It

DOES NOT fall like a curtain! I had to convince myself that the poet was just using a simile to make a point. It was just some amateurish poetic license. I had to convince myself that I didn't need to start carrying flashlights any time I was outdoors past noon. Nope. Night will not fall on me at one-thirty in the afternoon. Like a curtain.

OK, that was a bunch of fun talk about fear and darkness. But the fear is really not about darkness, it's about not having light. Light lets us see and lets us understand. Light is knowledge. It brings warmth. It is hope. It is the good in things. It is the good in us. Darkness doesn't have any of that.

It's probably shameful for a grown man to be afraid of the dark. I'd be embarrassed, except that over 2300 years ago, Plato gave me a pass. He said it like this. *"We can easily forgive a child who is afraid of the dark; the real tragedy of life is when men are afraid of the light."*

I'm not afraid of the light!

* * *

FEARS

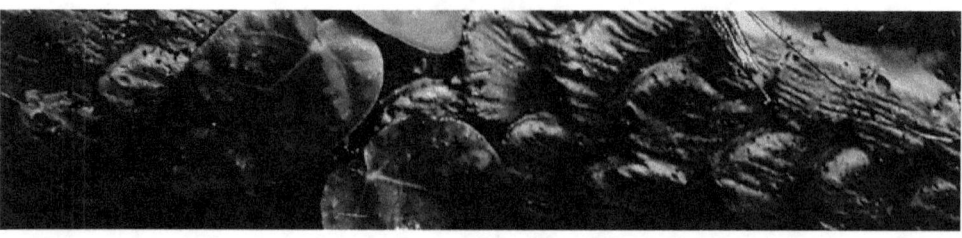

BILLIONS

23

BILLIONS

We are always surrounded by numbers and math. We often don't fully understand them, but they're always there. I am fortunate to have married a high school "mathlete" that wears her nerdiness well. So, I get a little help.

Last week the mathlete and I took the train over the mountains to Reno. When I'm home, at 40 feet elevation, the amount of oxygen in the air that I breathe is about 21%. Over the hill in Reno and Tahoe, the elevations are up to 6,000 feet. There, the oxygen in the air is 16.5%. The difference is only about 4.5%. Well, a slight dip of only 4.5% doesn't seem like much. But my mathlete tells me that there's actually 21.4% less available to my body. OK, that's significant. I don't understand it but thank you math! I certainly felt it.

On our way home, the train pulled over several times to meet oncoming trains and let them safely pass by in the occasional areas that had dual tracks. I know that somewhere, someone was charged with doing a whole lot of calculus, trigonometry, and algebra to determine how fast each train should go and where to pull over to avoid a collision. Again, I don't understand it all, but thank you math and numbers. We got home safely.

The biggest numbers problem that I've struggled with lately is to understand how big is a billion. More importantly, I'm trying to understand how rich is a billionaire. I've come to the conclusion that billionaires own everything, including our government. But I ask myself, how is that possible? It seems impossible, only because we don't really fully grasp how rich is a billionaire.

We tend to think that a billionaire is just a rich millionaire. But a billionaire IS NOT just a rich millionaire. The difference is a world apart. As an astonishing example, the mathlete told me that if a millionaire spent $1 per second, they'd run out of money in 12 days. But if a billionaire spent $1 per second, they could keep doing it for 31.7 years.! Wait!! What?? 12 days versus almost 32 years?!?! Yikes!

So, to make it a little easier to understand. A billionaire could give each and every sitting US senator a million dollars and barely scratch the surface of their pile of money. We've all heard that people will do some sketchy stuff for a Klondike bar, then imagine what a power and money-hungry politician would do for a million dollars.

There are over 600 billionaires in our country and over 135 private billion-dollar companies. The list continues to grow every day.

So how big is a billion? Here's my non-math description. If a millionaire is an eagle, then a billionaire is a sky-filling dragon that soars overhead, and its darkening shadow is so big that it can cover entire countries.

That's not just a big eagle!

* * *

KEEP ON BEING YOU

24

KEEP ON BEING YOU

I've often had nights where sleep just wasn't an option. As aggravating as it is, it's on those nights, alone in my easy chair, when I get in my deepest thinking.

On one of those sleepless nights I thought about how, throughout my life, there have been people around me that were so important to my journey. Of course, family are extremely important. My loving sisters, my cousins, heck, even my crazy brother carried me along. But I realized that there were always others.

When I was small, there were a handful of school friends. Later, in high school, I had a few other close friends. In my young adult life, there were some guys and gals and even a whole family helping me along. In college, I had some friends who helped me through. Even today, there are others, like the people at my work and my music friends. And of course, my dear Rhonda and our kids.

All of these people are very different. So, I sat and wondered, what did they all have in common? After some thought, I believe they all share a few traits that I've apparently needed during my life.

Each of these people has been supportive. But all of them were just critical enough to keep me growing. And each of them was gracious and understanding enough to be able to roll with my failures.

Those sleepless nights would have been just a fun trip down memory lane, until something exciting dawned on me. Sitting there in the dark, I realized that given the range of important people in my lifetime, both you and I are undoubtedly one of those people right now, to someone else. And we don't even realize it!

We don't realize that we are that person because it's not something we sign up for. We don't fill out applications. We don't wear a badge or have scheduled meetings. It's an honorary position. It just happens.

I can guarantee you that 50 years ago, Montie had no idea how his friendship shored me up when we were both just poor farm kids. Even today, I lean on him. Later on, there was Mark and Steve and then Ron and Rick and Larry and Leroy. The list goes on. Thirty years ago, Sarah or Jeff or Craig had no idea that I'd likely never have made it through my university time without them. Even now, but certainly since I recently had a big health scare, I've had people help me manage through many days. None of these folks were doing anything special, they were all just being there and being themselves!

So, I hope today, that I, and you, can recognize we are probably unknowingly very important to someone. Maybe it's in a minor way, or maybe it's in a major way. But it's probably unnoticed. So, I'll keep on being me and you just keep on being you. And I'll bet that somewhere in there, someone will someday look back on their life and think, I'm glad you were there!

* * *

FAMOUS LAST WORDS

25

FAMOUS LAST WORDS

In 1993, I graduated college. I barely graduated, but I graduated. My friends were all heading to grad school to become doctors. Not me. I grabbed the diploma out of the chancellor's hands and raced out of town before they could realize they might have made a grave mistake.

A short month later, I had achieved a dream. I was a wildlife biologist. It would be years before I was certified by The Wildlife Society, but I had a business card and it said right on the bottom – WILDLIFE BIOLOGIST. Looking back, I would confess that I wasn't much of one then. But I had just received that piece of paper from the University of California, Davis. The university had a well-respected program, and I was relying on their name, rather than my own, to get my career started.

During my senior year of college, I was hired as an intern to work on a 3,000-acre open-space and wildlife area, south of Sacramento. The area was called the Bufferlands. I was an intern, but that was just a hiring term. I worked for an engineer named Roy who had an office 30 miles away. I was the only person on the little refuge. I learned a lot from Roy, and he was a great guy, but he taught me zero about wildlife biology. There, I was on my own. My main role was to tend to 1000 trees that had been planted during an Earth Day event. My intern position allowed me to work 24 hours each week and I could arrange my own schedule. I could do it in the evenings, or weekends, or any way that I wished, so it was easy to work around my school schedule.

Some weeks, it took all of my 24 hours to keep the little trees watered. I had built a PVC water system and used a gas-powered pump to draw water from a lake. The water in the lake wasn't crystal clear. Far from it! So I spent many hours cleaning mud out of tiny water emitters I had placed at each of the 1000 trees. But most weeks, I was free to prowl around the area, take notes, and write in my sparkling new wildlife biology journal.

After I graduated, my boss asked me to stay and become a permanent and full-time employee. I had big dreams to travel and work in Alaska after I graduated. But this offer was a bird-in-the-hand moment, so I told him I would stay long enough to pay off my student loans. He had a longer view than I did, but he agreed to the deal. I signed some papers and the next week I had a full-time job with the County of Sacramento, the beginnings of a 401k, and best of all, I had business cards.

At first, I didn't have many responsibilities. I still took care of the little trees, but in addition, I was charged with planning a second tree planting for the coming fall. Even then, most of my time was spent roaming the area and documenting the interesting aspects of the ecology. Each day, I noted things like the number of beavers in the area and the trees that they were eating. I started a list of the birds I saw, and that list grew each day. I attended occasional meetings with my new contacts at the National Audubon Society. I met with others and discussed the possibilities the little refuge had to offer. It didn't take long for me to realize that the 3000-acre Bufferlands, surrounded by urban neighborhoods on three sides, was a unique property and could become a real gem to the whole area. It just needed a plan and a commitment to realize its potential.

Roy saw the potential too and wanted to promote the area's unique values even more than I did. During a meeting with him, I emphasized that before we could earnestly plan to enhance the area, we needed a reliable inventory of the plant and animal species, a detailed map of the habitats, and other ecological data. He asked if I was capable of leading the effort, assuming he could get approval to hire some help. I told him of course I was capable, it said Wildlife Biologist right there on my business card.

The truth is, I was nowhere near prepared for that role. But I had friends and contacts. While I was in school, I volunteered to help on various projects. PhD and Master's students always needed help with their research. Professors continually had flyers outside their offices, looking for assistants. I had helped them all. I gained a lot of experience in many aspects of ecology and wildlife biology, but more importantly, I made some friends and contacts. With crossed fingers, I would call in some favors.

During the next month, I sat at my desk, making phone calls and taking notes. Slowly, I outlined the survey protocol for each of the plant and animal groups. As I worked on the ecological side, Roy worked at getting the approvals to hire some interns. I had hoped we could get as many as ten. But Roy got approval for twelve. And though he knew little about biology, he was a genius when it came to the ins-and-outs of the county government's bureaucracy.

After a few months of head-scratching, pouring over wildlife textbooks, and calling in favors, I had a plan. Then I just needed the people. I drove back to my alma mater to spend the day recruiting help. I was fortunate that many of my classmates hadn't graduated yet and were still hungry students. Others had graduated, but some hadn't found jobs or moved away yet. I placed flyers in the career hall bulletin boards and left information with the career counselors that I knew. It was a paid position with potential for internship credits, so I was hopeful that within a week, I would have enough people to perform the work.

I got calls at work during the day and I got calls at my apartment at night. The jobs were temporary, so there wasn't a lot of red tape in the hiring process, and I had no problems hiring friends and people I knew. In short order, everything fell into place. I had a plan and enough people to begin the work. I had spent weeks getting fat at a desk. Now it was time to get outside and earn that Wildlife Biologist title.

We started by surveying birds. We would split into groups and visit different habitat types. Today, I know 300 birds by sight and almost as many just by their song. But back then, we all carried bird field guides and spent a lot of time arguing over pictures. It was fun work, and we got excited each time we would document a new bird to add to our growing list.

I managed to get a permit and we surveyed our lakes and streams for fish.

We learned how to use nets from the banks and how to use fish identification keys. In the coming months, we moved on to cataloging all the reptiles and amphibians. We learned how to install 50' long drift-fences that blocked the travel of snakes, lizards, toads, and frogs. As the little creatures traveled along the fence, they would fall into buried buckets and become trapped. It was exciting to check the buckets each morning and see what new animal was being added to our list.

When the time came for us to create a list of the area's mammals, it proved to be the most difficult. Plants, trees, and almost every bird species are out and visible during the daylight. But most of the mammals are only active at night. Even more troubling, many are highly secretive. Larger mammals, like deer or coyotes, can be seen or heard, but smaller mammals, like mice and voles, must be trapped.

Our small mammal surveys followed a fairly standard method we had all done once, during a field course at school. It involved setting hundreds of small box-shaped live-traps and then checking them each hour throughout the night. When we captured an animal, we would transfer it from the trap into a plastic bag. Using a small hanging scale, we would get the little animal's weight. The tricky part was to maneuver the little furry creatures into a corner of the bag, and then reach in and grab it by the scruff of the neck. Using head lamps and flashlights in the dark, we would log the animal's species, weight, sex, and then mark its belly with a bit of Miss Clairol roll-on hair die. Then we would release the animal back where it was captured. The hair-dye markings allowed us to know if an animal was recaptured later.

There were times when half of the traps had an animal. There were house mice, deer mice, meadow voles, and occasionally tiny little shrews with long pointy noses. On many occasions, it was a race to get all the captured animals processed and released and then get to the next area within the hour.

Working all night with a bunch of college friends was fun. Between trapping runs, we sat around on tailgates and talked. We made toe-curlers, the traditional biologist's hors d'oeuvres, for nighttime work. Ritz crackers, peanut butter and horse radish. At daylight, someone would drive into town and get doughnuts or breakfast burritos. If it was Friday morning, we would all drive into a nearby diner and have breakfast. This was the type of lighthearted summer that every person someday looks back on when they talk about "the good ol' days."

Well, the good ol' days abruptly ended with a phone call from a veterinarian friend. She informed us that a virus had been found in New Mexico and that it was potentially deadly. She explained it had already killed 13 people and over half of the people who got it had died. She ended by telling us that the virus was called Sin Nombre, a type of Hantavirus, and that it was possibly spread by deer mice.

We had trapped and handled over a hundred deer mice every night, and sometimes over a thousand every week. The vet informed us that the Centers for Disease Control had recommended we stop our work until there was more information on the new virus and they could develop safety protocol for handling deer mice, the potential carrier.

With this news, our fun-filled nights of small mammal trapping were over. We said goodbye to our midsummer nights of bonhomie. We had a lot of data and none of us wanted to catch a disease that entered your lungs, causing your blood vessels to leak and your lungs to fill up with fluid. None of us wanted to die from a disease that we had never even heard of. A disease with a high mortality rate and no cure.

We monitored ourselves for the next few weeks, but no one got sick. A month later, we were contacted by a group that was working with the CDC to get blood samples from deer mice in areas outside of New Mexico to see if the virus was elsewhere. The group asked if we would be willing to go through a safety program, take some tests, get fitted for a full-face respirator, and then resume our trapping for a short period. Once we were outfitted, we would be trained on how to draw blood from the captured deer mice. The blood samples would be placed into hermetically sealed vials and transferred to them daily.

It was a lot to ask. The disease was scary. But several of us felt an obligation, especially those of us who now had Wildlife Biologist written in big letters on our business cards. Surely if we trapped enough animals and supplied enough blood, we could document that the virus was not in our area, and we could get back to enjoying the good ol' days.

The process of trapping the mice and taking the blood samples was laborious. Just months before, we were out trapping in tee shirts and jeans. During this round, still in the heat of summer, we were covered in white Tyvek suits, disposable latex gloves, and a full-faced dual-canister respirator.

Each mouse that we caught was weighed, measured, and identified as male or female. We would put them into an aquarium that was full of CO_2. After only a few seconds, they would be immobilized just long enough for us to put a tiny capillary tube, smaller than a toothpick, into the corner of their eye. The capillary action of the minuscule tube would draw out a small amount of blood. We placed each tube into a vial, labeled each one, and placed them into a rack.

It was brutal work. The suits were hot, and it was difficult to spend long hours breathing through the respirators. At the end of each shift, we were exhausted. We had red lines on our faces from the masks, and our clothes were soaked from sweat. Everything that we touched or used had to be wiped down with disinfectant at the end of every shift. We wiped every flashlight, clipboard, and ink pen. We had a chart to show us how to wash our hands properly. We were introduced to a new product called hand sanitizer.

After a few months, much was learned about Hantavirus. It *was* spread by deer mice, and it *was* found in mice here in California. It was not prevalent, like it was elsewhere, but it was definitely here. We learned that it was primarily spread by breathing dust contaminated by the mouse's urine and feces. The greatest risk was from deer mice living in your house or when cleaning out sheds and buildings that had mice living there.

It was welcome news for those of us who had Wildlife Biologist at the bottom of our business cards. We would still have to be careful, but we could look forward to more of the good ol' days. We could toss out all of the white suits and lab gloves and bottles of disinfectant. We would never again wear face masks. We would put this scare behind us and never have to worry about a deadly virus again.

Famous last words.

* * *

RHONDA

26

RHONDA

I've had plenty of times in my life when I've been in the right place, at the wrong time. I'm the guy that gets pulled over for speeding when I'm just rolling along with the flow of traffic. Every car around me is going the exact same speed, but there I am, sitting on the side of the road, with flashing blue lights in my mirror. I'm the poor guy that's just waiting for the long arm of the law to walk back and stick a fat ticket through my window and tell me to have a nice day.

I could go on. Right place. Wrong time. But I don't want to talk about fist fights and black eyes. I'd rather not bring up a pistol pointed in my direction. I don't want to even mention about a pine cone falling from a 100-foot tree. Right place. Wrong time. Ouch.

I want to talk about love. I want to talk about the love of my life. I want to talk about my one experience with being at the right place at the right time.

In the mid-90s I used to spend some evenings at America Live, in Sacramento's Downtown Plaza. The sprawling, two-story complex had a sports Bar with a boxing ring dance floor, a country music line-dancing bar, a comedy club, a dueling piano bar, several restaurants, and a little spot called Jackass Flats.

I spent a lot of time at The Flats. I wasn't much interested in Karaoke, but a couple of nights a week, they had open-mic night. I tried to never miss one. I was a shy guitar player, so I went and studied each performer. I watched guys like Roadkill Ray pick and sing. I watched ladies sing and play so effortlessly, that it seemed their guitars were just a part of their body. I saw guys strum so hard that I watched for pieces of their guitar to go flying in the air. I got to see performers across the whole spectrum of styles and experience. I saw a few performers that were probably as bad as me, but they had nerve. Everyone got a cheerful round of applause.

Whenever my oldest and dearest friend Montie was going to be in town, he would meet me at the Flats at seven o'clock. Then, we'd walk down a floor to Gatlin's country bar. He and I had spent a lifetime of hanging out. We had great times. We had fished and camped together our whole lives. But at that point in time, many of our fun times ended with a hangover.

One particularly memorable night in June, I sat there at The Flats waiting on Montie, and glanced at my watch. Eight o'clock. For all of his fun, he was a little undependable in his scheduling. But I didn't have anything else to do. So, I'd just walk downstairs and wait. I headed that way. Even in the stairway, I could hear the loud country music booming through the walls.

I found an empty spot at the bar and ordered a Coors Light. The bartender sat it on the counter and took my money. I spun my stool around to get a look. It was a Friday night, and the place was getting packed. I scanned across the sea of wannabe cowgirls on the dance floor. Line dancing was popular and there was every size, shape and age of men and women, stomping their feet, spinning and dipping, and doing whatever line dancers did.

I looked further around the room, and down the bar. I nodded at girls smiling at me. I smiled at girls nodding at me. There were groups of guys standing around, drinking whiskeys and hoping to get lucky. There were groups of girls scattered around, dressed in their Daisy Dukes or skirts and cowboy boots. They all looked alike, and I'd seen a million of them. I never put much effort into the whole scene. I knew that if I just sat back and watched, as soon as they all had a few Tequila shots, a group of the girls would come over and start some talk. So, I did just that. The place was a meat market and most everyone was there for the same reason. Or close to it anyway.

I scanned around a dozen more cute faces, red lipstick, and tight-ass jeans. Every girl in the place was just a slight variation of the ones on each side, and each trying to out-sexy the next. I'm not complaining, I was just past 30 years old, fresh out of college, and as red-blooded as any male in the world. I'm just trying to adequately paint a mental picture of Gatlin's, Sacramento, on a Friday night, 1994.

As I drank my beer, I continued to look around the squirming sea of bodies. But just like on a Saturday morning cartoon, my eyes did a screeching stop and backed up. The DJ had just started a new song and a big group of people had headed to the dance floor. Left behind and in my full view was the sweetest little blonde gal that I had ever seen. And she was looking *at me*!

I looked back to make sure there wasn't some six-foot tall, lantern-jawed, boot model cowboy standing behind me. There wasn't. She *was* smiling at me. I smiled back. But as quickly as the space had emptied, it refilled with bodies, and she was gone from my sight.

Well, my passive *sit and wait* game was over. I stood up and walked in her direction, but by now the place was packed. I leaned from side to side to see past people, but there was nothing. Just more cloned cowgirls and horny guys.

I managed to make my way back to the bar seat before it was gone. I continued to look around and before long, I saw her again. She was with a girlfriend, on the dance floor, doing some kind of "boot scoot boogie" thing. I didn't pay much attention to her friend, but I watched the little blonde dance. She had a different vibe than any other girl in the place. She looked fun and wholesome and far less *hey cowboy let's go out to the parking lot.* She stuck out.

When the song ended, I was standing at the edge of the dance floor, ready to punch any drunk that got in my way. To leave the dance floor, she'd have to pass right by me. I stood while the sea of boots passed by, but there was no her. The DJ started another song, and I looked up to see her and her friend, waiting on the dance floor for another dance. She was in the front, now only a few feet from me. I nodded and she motioned for me to come and dance next to her.

Well, damn! I wasn't prepared for that. I just wanted to talk, not dance. No one can dance on only one beer. Granted, a couple of Jägermeister shots and you'd swear I was in a "Dance Dance Revolution" contest. But I wasn't ready.

I quickly listened to the song and watched the dancer's feet. It looked pretty simple. It was the Electric Slide, the only line dance that I had ever attempted (again, it was only after some shots). But I sensed a *now or never* moment and hastily jumped in beside her. If I pulled it off, I would look good. If not, I just hoped that there were points for trying.

Within just a few beats, I was sliding and dipping right beside her. We laughed together when I messed up, went the wrong way, and bumped sides with her. We smiled at each other every time we turned around and faced each other. The song was three and a half minutes long, and I already had a comfortableness with her. I was doomed.

After the song was over, I grabbed her waist and led her to a quieter corner so that we could talk.

I reached out my hand.

"I'm Rawge" I said with my nicest smile.

"I'm Rhonda" she said with an even nicer smile and the cutest hint of a southern accent.

"Where you from?"

"Alabama, but I live here now. How about you? "

"I'm from down in the San Joaquin Valley. But I live here now, too."

Her name was Rhonda. I could end here and just say, well, I was finally in the right place at the right time, and the rest is history. But there's a lot more to this story. A lot more.

We talked and joked and even danced a few more times. It was easy and comfortable. I thought up funny things to say, just to hear her cute giggle. It was too loud to have much of a real conversation, so we didn't ask a lot of questions about each other. We just laughed and watched drunk people and cowboys trying to get lucky. When it got late, Rhonda's friend was ready to go home. But I wasn't ready to stop looking into her blues eyes.

"Hey, let's go get breakfast. I can give you a ride home."

"Ha. Nice try. I don't do that."

"You don't eat breakfast?

"Well... I don't do 'breakfast'." She emphasized the air quotes.

Before I could try to convince her that I truly wanted breakfast and a chance to sit down and have a real conversation, she turned and told me that if I wanted to see her again, she'd be at the river the next day at noon, at the little beach by Garcia Bend. She said that she'd be there with her two kids. She glanced back and said, "Maybe I'll see you tomorrow." Then she disappeared through the doors.

On my short drive home, I thought about Rhonda's parting words... *I'll be there with my two kids.* I thought about how I lived with a lingering feeling that I was behind. It nagged me day and night. When I had started college, I had been out of high school for almost seven years. The kids in my freshman class were seven years younger than I was, so the kids that I graduated with were also seven years younger. By the time they were my age, they would all have jobs and wives and husbands and bank accounts. They'd surely have nice cars and nice credit scores and would be buying houses. I had none of that. I was behind even as I started. The thought of a relationship with a woman and a couple of little kids didn't affect me the way Rhonda probably thought it would.

The next day at noon I was headed to Garcia Bend. I had never been there, but I knew where it was. I passed by it, on the opposite side of the river, every day on my way to work. I drove past it and continued five miles to the only bridge on the river, then headed back on the other side. I found my way to the Bend and parked. There were about fifty people, sitting or laying on beach towels, scattered around the sand. I stood and looked from group to group, hoping to see them, without having to wander around. No one looked familiar, so I started walking through the sand.

I hadn't gone far when I heard her. "Hey!"

I turned to see her smiling face.

"You showed up!"

"Of course I did! You ain't getting rid of me that easy!"

She motioned and I sat down beside her in the sand. It wasn't hard to miss two little blonde-haired kids staring up at me. One was a towheaded little boy, about four, and the other was a slightly older little girl, with a mop of long hair. Levi and Teresa. I had no idea then, but I was destined to say those names a million times.

After only fifteen minutes, Levi was my buddy. Teresa made it plain that I'd have to work hard for her approval or attention. Levi and I splashed in the water, threw beach balls, and had fun. Teresa sat by Rhonda and watched. Rhonda watched us, too. I couldn't stay long, as I had to go into work. Before I left, Rhonda asked me to drive up to their house for lunch or dinner, the next day. It was about 40 miles away, up into the foothills, so she gave me directions. I told her that I'd try to be there around four o'clock.

I found her house in the hills, on a little creek. We had dinner, I played catch with Levi, we talked until dark, and I went home. If that evening was going into my diary, I might mention the delicious, but modest home-cooked meal. I might mention Levi's little attitude when I threw a bad wiffleball pitch and he had to run and get the stray ball. I might mention Teresa was still watching it all, with a hint of scowl on her face. But more than likely, I'd write about eyes so blue they'd make the sky jealous. I would surely scribble about a smile that could make a grown man's heart take a few extra beats.

But I'm sure that I'd write about a first kiss and then end with drawing a bunch of hearts. But I don't write in diaries. I'm a grown man.

Dinners at her house became my routine. I'd get off work and head for her place. It was exciting and it was fun. Rhonda was incredible. This isn't the place for details, but she rocked my world. I had never known a woman like her, and we became closer each day. I learned of her early life and her move to Sacramento. She told me of her divorce and the kids' absent biological father. I learned of her struggles as a single mom.

The struggles weren't told to me. I saw them myself. I saw them each day as she raced from work to daycare to pick up the kids, and then home to make dinner and get homework done. I saw them when she woke up at 4 a.m. to get the kids ready, get them to school, and then drive down the hill to get to work on time. There were times when her car wouldn't start, and a new battery would have to wait until payday. There were times when one of the kids was sick and her boss had a fit if she had to miss a day of work. She struggled, but she was as tough as she was pretty. She made it work.

It didn't take long before I knew that Rhonda was terribly smart. She seemed to be able to do just about anything and loved the challenge of figuring something out. Nothing was beyond her. She thought deep. She had dreams, and most of all, she had plans. She knew where she wanted to be and knew that she would get there. Some of it seemed a long way off, but her tiny little frame was bursting full of determination. She was going to have a wonderful life, and nothing would stop her.

I wanted that too. But I didn't have a plan. I wanted in on Rhonda's plan. I needed in on Rhonda's plan! I had catching up to do.

Somewhere in that time, there was an "I love you." A month or so later, I even got the courage to say it. But once that was on the table, life took off. Rhonda and the kids moved in with me and we shared life's duties. The kids called me Rawge, out of habit, but I was their dad. We took a vow to never say stepdad. We took them to outdoor concerts and cultural events. We worked on science fair projects and wrestled with homework. All the while, Rhonda and I became more in love.

In 1996, we decided to try to buy a house. We got approved for a loan of $100,000 and would need $3,000 for a down payment. We saved every penny that we could and worked any overtime that we could get. But Rhonda quickly settled into an idea. She and I had worked in our garage and built our four-poster canopy bed and a matching blanket chest. We didn't have much money, but we built it cheaply using reclaimed lumber we bought from a guy who advertised in the local PennySaver, a weekly want-ad magazine. If we could build five or six more, and sell them in the PennySaver, we would have a down payment.

So, we spent our evenings building beds. We would sit in our little duplex garage, with the door open, and argue about measurements and drawing lines. We'd cut boards and dream about someday having electric chop saws and screw guns. Together, we would saw, nail, screw (get your mind out of the gutter), and build. Depending on the amount of pleasant "arguing," we'd complete a bed and chest every two or three weeks. They were beautiful. We were always surprised to see each one sell in only a few days. We would take the money, pull out a little for materials or tools for the next bed, and then put the rest away. In only 6 months, we had enough money for a down payment. The money was great, but that time had an extra bonus. We learned that we could work together. We looked into the future and saw us buying an old house and knowing that we could spend the rest of our lives, rebuilding it into anything that we wanted.

After spending a month driving around with a real estate agent, we found a house. We dropped our little wad of bed-making money and moved to Elverta. The house was rundown, but it had a bedroom for each of us and two bathrooms. It had a full acre for the kids to play and ride bikes, and some space for us to grow. There was room to plant a garden and an orchard. It was built the year that I was born, so every room needed an upgrade. We didn't care. It was ours, and we had a lifetime to make it exactly what we wanted.

The "new" house was only 15 minutes away from where we had lived, but as old as it was, everything was new. We had a new house, the kids had new bedrooms and new schools, and Rhonda and I had something new, too. Before, we had pieces of my life and pieces of her life, but once we moved, everything was our life.

A year or so after we moved to Elverta, life was wonderful. The house was slowly looking better. The kids had settled into their new schools and had neighborhood friends. They rode bikes and made forts. Rhonda and I loved each other and fell asleep each night on a handmade bed, in a freshly painted bedroom, and whispered sweet dreams to each other.

One beautiful evening, while the kids were with friends, Rhonda and I were eating at a Mexican restaurant, at an outdoor table with a cool evening breeze. We sat and talked about whatever passed through our minds. We talked about work. We chatted casually about the world. The conversation was as light as the Delta breeze that kept Sacramento cool at night. Life was good and I wouldn't change a thing.

"I wish we were married."

Hearing those words come out of Rhonda's red lips and into our lighthearted conversation was like a needle scratch on an old record. I instantly wrinkled my forehead and launched into, "We don't need to be married! It's just a damn piece of paper! I'm not getting married again! It didn't work out for me, and it didn't work out for you! I'm just not."

I folded my arms and sat back in my chair. I looked up and saw something in Rhonda's beautiful blue eyes, something that I'd never seen before. I had seen the look of determination. I had seen the look of glee. I had seen the look of love, many times. But I had never seen them cry. I had never seen them overflow with disappointment. In an instant, my heart sank.

Only a moment before, I wouldn't change a thing. A moment later, everything was changed. My heart had hit bottom and it would never be the same. I ended the conversation saying that we would talk about it later. But that was a white lie. We wouldn't talk about it later. We wouldn't need to. I would fix it.

Over the coming days and weeks, I thought about that conversation. I thought about it during the day, and I fell asleep at night thinking about what I had said. I wondered how I could have been so unaware. I thought about Rhonda having to introduce me as her boyfriend. I thought about papers and signatures with different names. But mostly, I thought about blue eyes with tears.

On Valentine's Day in 1998, I made a vow to myself that I would spend the rest of my life making up for ...well for ...well for whatever I was before that moment. I would never be party to another tear in Rhonda's eyes, and Lord have mercy on the poor soul of anyone else that does. That morning, I proposed. It wasn't the grandest proposal in the history of mankind, but at that moment we became fiancés. In just a few short months, we would be husband and wife.

In September, we had a small wedding in our backyard. Rhonda cooked a chili verde dinner for the guests. A friend donated tables, chairs, and tablecloths from his business. An old friend from my old home town donated wine and drinks. Some of Rhonda's friends decorated and brought flowers. My friend Montie was my best man and he showed up on time. That night, we were Mr. and Mrs. Jones.

Our marriage was the inflection point in our lives. We hardly even noticed as Rhonda moved up through her company to become a top salesperson. I also moved up quickly, becoming a senior in my job class. Soon we attended a local church and brought that part of our childhoods into our kids' lives. Rhonda drew from her younger years in high school jazz band and choir and started playing music in church. She played keys and sang. I played guitar. That experience cinched us as a team. Rawge and Rhonda. R&R became a word.

We quickly went from waiting on payday to it just being another day in the week. Life changed and although we hardly noticed it, there wasn't much denying that each day got better. There were problems and even catastrophes, but R&R could handle it.

On Valentine's Day 25 years later, here I sit in a beautiful foreign country, struggling to put our wonderful and love filled lives into words. But I realize, this is a never-ending story. I want to write how fortunate I've been to watch Rhonda smile when she put on a $10 cotton dress that I had given her, and later seeing that same smile when she put on her first strand of pearls. I feel like I should describe how beautiful she looks in an evening gown at a gala or how peaceful she looks in a boho dress, picking flowers in the yard. If I had nothing but time and words, I'd describe how confident she looks, sitting at her desk, staring at a computer screen full of data with 30 windows open.

But I don't have the time or the words. It's Valentine's Day. It's time to dress up and stare into each other's eyes. It's almost time to sit down for dinner, toast a white wine and listen to the monkeys howl in the jungle. I need to hurry, it's almost time to sit and giggle about our memories on this day, around the world. Memories in Elverta. Memories in Barcelona. We'll toast about a hot Valentine's night in Cabo San Lucas and a breezy night in Maui. Then we'll open a second bottle and toast to all the Valentine's days to come and dream of where we might be.

Tonight, I'll fall asleep without the feeling that I'm behind. And tomorrow we'll wake up to add pages to our never-ending story. But I'm told that no one likes a story with no end. So, I'll end with this...

Someday, when I'm down to my last breath, I'll be torn between holding it, to get one last minute of staring into Rhonda's beautiful eyes or using it for one last kiss on her red lips.

* * *

RHONDA

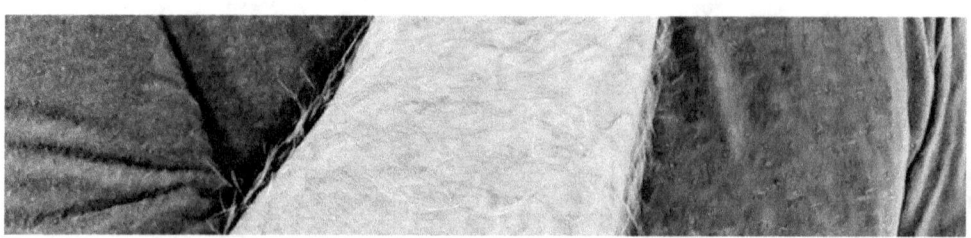

EPIPHANY!

27

EPIPHANY!

I 've had three epiphanies in my life. One is too personal to talk about. One was when I went to sleep one night as a tough guy and woke up in the hospital, a handicapped old man. The other one was quite a few years ago and my life changed in a moment. That one is worth talking about.

I was driving my 30-minute commute from work in my Toyota pickup. I had NPR playing on the radio, but it was mostly background noise. I wasn't paying it much attention until I heard the word "median," and my ears perked up. I'm a big fan of the median as a statistical tool. I've complained many times that the world has embraced the average because it's far easier to calculate. To make my point, just take some data and throw in a few outlier high or low numbers and the average suddenly is a bad representative. The median handles this much better – just ask any real estate agent.

This particular NPR segment was talking about the lifespan of Americans. When it told the median life expectancy of an American male, the number kind of startled me. I was half that age. The number they gave was very precise. 76.58 years. I did some more math in my head, and it seemed that I was *exactly* half of that age. I was so freaked out, that I pulled off to the side of the road, threw my glove box open and fumbled through junk until I found my cheap little calculator (this was way before smart phones). I flipped my visor down and peeled off the little advertising calendar that was stuck underneath. As quickly as I could, I started counting days and pushing buttons. I changed my age into days, subtracted for my birthday, divided by 365 to get an actual decimal, and so on. No matter what math I did, the answer said that I was 38.29 years old. Yes, at that very moment I was *exactly* one half of my predicted life span!

Of course, this rocked my world. How could this be? Where did the time go? I've got so much more I want to accomplish! I'll never have time! Heck, given the report cards that the kids were bringing home, it'd likely take 30 years just to get them out of the house! I haven't traveled. I haven't written a book. I haven't mastered guitar. I haven't gotten my 6-pack abs! My mind was racing through all the things I'd yet to do.

I got home and Rhonda instantly saw a distressed look on my face and asked, "What's wrong with you? "

I told her "I'm exactly half dead, that's what's wrong with me!"

Of course, the revelation had rattled me and sent me into a lot of thinking and reminiscing. When you're sitting at what you perceive as the zenith of your life, it's a nice spot to look both forward and back. It's like being on the top of a mountain. You can see everything. Looking back, you can really see and embrace the beautiful memories. But looking forward from that spot, it's all blank. But you know that somewhere out there is the end. The final dot on your timeline. And it's getting closer with every breath!

I eventually reasoned that since the whole bomb seemed to be dropped on me from the cosmos via an NPR segment, there must be a positive message in there somewhere! There must be a reason for that pointed knowledge. It consumed me for a while. But soon I realized that what was in front of me, be it long or short, was 100% opportunity. What was behind me was done and written, but in front of me was nothing but wide open space, ready to be lived and created. I slowly stopped looking at the impending horizon and started looking down. Down was today and I needed to grab it!

Since then, I have really tried to seize every day. Yes, I still plan for the future, but I don't let a day go by that I don't try to wring every drop of enjoyment out of it. I'm fortunate that Rhonda has the same spirit. When we do look toward the horizon, it's not to see if the end is getting closer, but to see what we can plan next! No one is promised tomorrow, and age is just a number.

Carpe Diem, my friends!

* * *

REBORN GUITARS

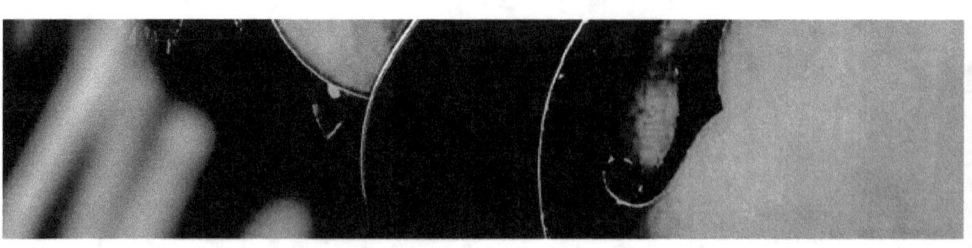

28

REBORN GUITARS

One afternoon, my son Levi and I had taken a load of junk to the county dump. This was rare, but even when you live by the "three Rs" rule, Reduce—Reuse—Recycle, at some point you still end up with a pile of junk. We had loaded up the bed of my big black Dodge truck and were backed into a bay at the dump. We had already taken all our metal pieces to the metal recycling area and any wood to the wood chipping area. Now we were at the heart of the dump – the smelly garbage area.

As I stood in the back of the truck, kicking out the last of our items, I took a minute to look around at what others were throwing away. When I was a kid and we went to the dump, you could walk around and pick stuff up. Farm kids mostly prowled around, kicking through boxes of dirty magazines, and finding an occasional bike frame or something useful. But here, you stayed in your lane and didn't touch anything. I shook my head as I saw people tossing out stuff that could have been given away or reused. But this is America, in the year 2000, and we don't do that much anymore.

In the back of the huge metal warehouse, a big loader machine was pushing the hills of garbage towards a conveyor belt that loaded it all into big trucks. The trucks carried it to its eternal home and buried it. The dumps live by the adage – out of sight, out of mind. As I watched the loader pushing a mountain of garbage ahead of it, I shivered as I saw an acoustic guitar tumbling along in front of the rolling pile. The guitar made a few tumbles and then was squashed by the heap. It disappeared beneath the pile and was gone.

I winced at the thought of someone throwing away a guitar. But before I could give it much thought, I was jarred back to reality by a blaring horn from someone that wanted me to get busy and get out of the way. I jumped down, closed my tailgate, and rolled up the knotted ropes that we had used to tie down our load. I started my truck and got out of the way of the impatient horn man and headed back home.

As I made the fifteen minute drive home, I thought and wondered why someone would throw away a guitar. Were they just cleaning out a closet and had no place else to put it? The more I thought about it, I wondered if there was a guitar or other musical instrument in every closet in America. I imagined that every family, at some point, had a kid who wanted to learn to play an instrument. I knew from some experience that 99% of them give up and whatever instrument the parents managed to get their hands on was probably relegated to the closet.

For the next few weeks, the thought of millions of guitars wasting away in America's closets floated around in my mind. Back then, I had two guitars – one that I played and one that I loaned out. The one I loaned out had electronics built into it and there was always someone waiting to borrow it. Those two thoughts finally gelled into an idea – I would make it my mission to get guitars out of people's closets and into the hands of people who need them. With that thought, Reborn Guitars was born!

For the next several months, I started asking around for guitars in closets. Every Saturday morning, I cruised the local yard sales and flea markets. I bought every beat-up guitar that I could find. I enrolled in the YouTube School of Luthiers and Guitar Repair. OK, there's no such thing, but I spent every spare moment watching guitar repair videos. I learned how to use steam to remove a neck from the body, by practicing on a $10 Yamaha. I learned how to repair cracks on a guitar that someone had stepped on. I learned how to replace and restore frets on a guitar that someone had played to death. I devoured the learning and fell in love with working in my little guitar shop.

Today I can do most any repair. I can install electronics and add beautiful pearl inlays. I have even built several electric guitars from scratch. I have given away hundreds of guitars and other instruments. There are Reborn Guitars being played all over our country and around the world. I have a collection of photos of people with their new guitars and all of them showing someone with a huge smile on their face.

Most of the instruments were purchased by me at auctions, yard sales, and such, but I have gotten quite a few instruments from people's closets. Hardly a month goes by that I don't get a call or message from someone asking if I want an old instrument they've had lying around. I've received some cool stuff, ranging from guitars and ukuleles, to banjos and fiddles. I've rebuilt autoharps and dulcimers and other instruments that aren't extremely popular, but I still found homes for them.

One day I got a phone call from a lady who had gotten my number from a friend of a friend. She told me she had an accordion in her closet and was wondering if I might want it. I told her that sadly, I did not want it. I went further to let her know that I knew nothing about them or how they even worked, and that in 20 years, no one had ever approached me about needing one. I thanked her for thinking of me and then ended by encouraging her to play it or take some lessons.

Years prior, I had purchased an accordion on eBay. Rhonda plays piano and keyboard, so I thought it would be really cute to watch her play an accordion. She's really musically talented and I figured that she could pick up the basics in no time at all. When it arrived, it was so big and heavy that Rhonda couldn't even hold it. It had a thick leather harness, but no matter how we adjusted it, she would fall over the moment I let go of it. So, like so many other instruments, it was sent to the back of a dusty closet.

A few years later, I met a guy who played the accordion and just loved it. He had traveled the country, performing at polka events. I got to hear him play and he was incredible. I mentioned to him that I had one at home, gathering dust in a closet and asked him if he had any use for it. I would be happy to give it to him. He graciously declined and told me that he already had several at home. He ended our conversation by telling me the following true story.

I was playing a polka festival in a big city. When I arrived, I parked my car on the street, in front of the hotel where I was staying, and walked to the front desk to check in. Once I had the key, I took my suitcase and made my way to the elevator. The door closed and I started up to the top floor. As I traveled up, I suddenly realized that I had left my car with the window down and left my accordion in the back seat.

In a panic, I started pushing buttons to try to get the elevator turned around. I finally succeeded and when the doors opened, I ran across the lobby and out to the street. Out of breath, I skidded up to the open window of my car. But it was too late.

There were already three other accordions in there.

The gentleman went on to tell me that there must be a million accordions gathering dust in closets, because he gets offered an accordion at most every gig.

So, I'll just hang on to the grand piano-sized accordion, in the refrigerator-sized case that takes up most of our closet. Surely someday I'll stumble onto a shop called Reborn Accordions, and they'll just love to take it off my hands!

* * *

CHARACTER FLAWS

29

CHARACTER FLAWS

I t seems that there's always something coming along to make me aware of a personal character flaw. From the day we're born, we are taught the difference between right and wrong. But even early on, we start realizing that it's not all black and white. Then we spend the rest of our lives navigating the dangerous gray areas. The gray areas are where we show our character.

I know how I'd respond if I was ever robbed. Let's say I walked up to a counter and ordered a cup of coffee "to go." A man tells me it'll be three dollars. After I hand him the money, he grabs a pot and pours the coffee on the counter. Then he drops a paper cup on it.

This is where all that "use your words" training comes into play. I'm sure that I'd simply demand he try it again but put the cup down first. If that didn't happen, then I'd demand my money back. If that didn't work, well, most of my *right and wrong* training would probably just go out the window and some of my character would start showing through. If the guy wasn't more than twice my size, I'd probably take three dollars out of his hide. If he was bigger than me, he'd at least get a quick kick in the sweet spot. I wouldn't get my money back, but I'd soothe some inner injustice.

Let's say I ordered a bag of chips at the same counter. I wonder how I'd react if he just dangled the bag of chips, just out of my reach, and said "Oh look, they're stuck." Heck, I'd probably just skip the "use your words" part and go straight into the ass kicking.

But here's where some of that gray area really happens. What if it's a machine that's robbing me? What if I put $3 into a machine that dispensed the coffee, let it spill all over, and then it drops out a cup? What if after I wadded up the empty cup and threw it towards the trash can, I wanted coffee so badly that I did it a second time, with the same result?

I've just been robbed of six hard-earned dollars by a brainless machine. Is it all on me for being dumb enough to do it twice? Or does it justify a good solid kick to its tender plexiglass? I wouldn't get my money back, but again, I'd soothe some inner injustice.

Hmm. Gray area?

Rhonda, my constant voice of reason, shakes her pretty head and says "Just walk away, tough guy. Every time we're in Las Vegas, there's machines that take a lot more than six measly dollars from you. You never haul off and kick one of them!"

She's right, but it's not like it never crossed my mind. I guess my fine and upstanding character really shines when I'm surrounded by casino security. Much less so, at a highway rest area in the middle of the night.

But I'm working on it.

* * *

LONG HAIR

30

LONG HAIR

I like my hair. Yep, it's a bit long for a man and is usually just begging for a brush. But after 35+ years, it's just become a recognizable part of who I am.

Of course, having long hair has come with some issues. I've had more than my share of jokes and overheard whispers. But I can handle it. If you want to look like a girl, you've got to be at least a little tough. You know, kind of like *A Boy Named Sue.* Well, not quite that tough, but at least expect the occasional ribbing and be ready to take it.

My favorite story of my long hair woes happened about 10 years ago. Rhonda and I were car shopping and walked onto a car lot. We were looking at a car, when behind us, I heard a couple of salesmen step outside the door of their office. One of them told the other, "You go over there." Then I saw him point toward us and say, "I'm gonna go over and talk to those two ladies."

Well, I didn't *hit him hard right between the eyes* and we didn't end up crashing *through the mud and the blood and the beer.* Nope. Like any respectable and civilized man, I used my words.

When he walked over, I politely told him, "Us two ladies are gonna shop elsewhere before one of us two ladies decides to whoop somebody's ass!"

He muttered, "Fair enough." And we left. No sale for that guy!

* * *

OUR BUBBLES

31

OUR BUBBLES

There was a time in my life when every person around me was just like me. They all thought like me and looked like me. They all told me exactly what I wanted to hear and confirmed anything I wanted to say. I got my news from one source and that news also told me what I wanted to hear. I stuck pretty close to home. I didn't read much, and I locked the gate at night. I was comfortable, and I was fine with it, inside my bubble.

We all live in a bubble.

But we don't all live in the same sized bubble.

Our bubbles are defined by the people, places, events, ideas, and thinking that surrounds us and influences us.

I've grown to know that the larger the bubble, the more we can relate to others. The more we can relate to others, the more we can love others. The more we can love others, the more we can serve others. The more we can serve and help and add positive things into the world, the happier we are.

But, when we put restrictions on the value and size of those people, events, places, ideas, and thinking that surrounds us, our precious bubbles get smaller and smaller. Small bubbles can quickly lead to a bunch of those words that end in "ism". Small bubbles tend to push our ideas and notions to their extreme ends. I've seen it in myself and others. I've seen it in areas ranging from religion to politics, and about everything in between.

There's nothing funny about extremism and radicalism. But to keep it light, here's a fun and farcical example. Let's say that someone's favorite color is red. They decorate their house in red and occasionally wear a red shirt. One day someone tells them how great they look in red. So, they start dressing more in red. Soon they meet someone else that lives and dresses in red and they start hanging out. After a bit, there's a small group of them who hang out to discuss the beauty and benefits of red.

But before long, they start looking around at people that don't wear red and wonder what is wrong with them? They distance themselves from the non-red people and secretly (at first) call them names.

The real issues start when the non-red people become their enemy. The red-only people convince each other that red is something superior. They watch a guy on YouTube that has "evidence" that wearing red can cure diseases. They watch another guy who explains how wearing red comes straight out of a holy book, if you just read it correctly. They watch another guy who tells them it's all true but that the government and "mainstream" media just don't want you to know. They believe it all because they tell each other it's true. Soon, they won't tolerate anything that's not red and will defend red to the point of violence. They become mean and post nasty things on social media. You know, the ones we see that start with "Wake Up People!"

I'm sure you get my point. That's what happens with a small bubble. Again, I know, because I've been there.

I was in college when I first realized how small my bubble was. Suddenly, I was surrounded by people who were different than me. In fact, almost no one was like me. It was scary at first, but after I started making new friends from different worlds, there was no denying that a bigger bubble felt good! Before long, I wanted it even bigger.

I must admit, enlarging your bubble sounds much easier than it is. Despite the rewards, getting a bigger bubble is a challenge. It's hard to get out of our little bubbles or to let someone else in. I was very fortunate that about 25 years ago, Rhonda grabbed me by the bubbles and said, "Come on! We've got places to go and people to meet." Since then, it's been eye-opening.

We both wanted a bubble where people thought differently than us and helped us see another perspective. We wanted a bubble where people even spoke a different language. We wanted a bubble where people had a different skin color, worshipped differently, and had different struggles. We wanted a bubble that had no borders.

We keep trying and learning. We keep making new friends. We keep growing.

It's worth noting that expanding our bubbles is not a new concept. Almost a hundred years before I was born, Mark Twain knew about bubbles. He wrote these words about travel:

"Travel is fatal to prejudice, bigotry, and narrow-mindedness, and many of our people need it sorely on these accounts. Broad, wholesome, charitable views of men and things cannot be acquired by vegetating in one little corner of the earth all one's lifetime."

I think his words are true, whether the travel is across the street, across the country or across the world.

Mark Twain was eloquent.

I'm less refined.

Bigger Bubbles are Better!

* * *

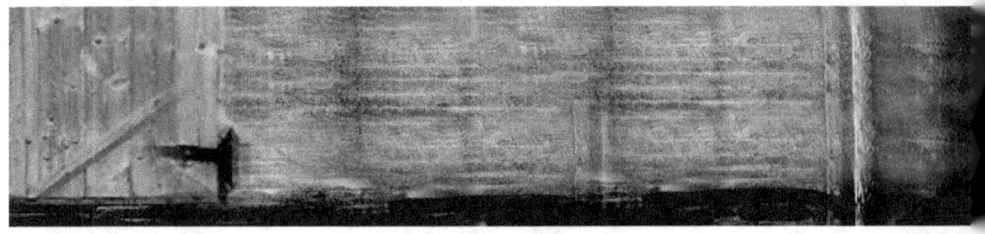

AGE

32

AGE

O
ne day, I was taking some photographs of a rustic old barn. It was
probably a hundred years old and hadn't been used in years. As
I walked around the old silos and strolled through the overgrown
farmyard, I couldn't help but think about the old barn's past. I couldn't help
but wonder, when was it at its most valuable service?

When it was young, I'm sure it was big and strong. The solid roof and walls
protected hay from the rain and seeds from the wind. The big solid doors
swung easily, and the farmer rested knowing his feed and future were safe.
That silent barn worked hard and stood tall.

Later, as the barn matured, its boards loosened, and the paint began to
fade. Sunlight began to trickle through the cracks. In a storm, the wind would
whistle and hiss through the rafters. The haystacks were moved to a dry corner
and the pallets of seed were covered with tarps. The doors were more often left
open as they sagged a bit and loudly complained each time they were swung.
Kids built seesaws with planks on the open floor and played *king of the hill* on
the stack of hay. Though the roof's peaks and beams were bowed, that barn
stood and continued to work hard.

Today, the barn has aged into a landmark. The sun has turned the wood a
beautiful brown. Wind and weather have given the beams and boards a texture
that can be felt. The glass is splintered and mostly gone from the windows.
Their traces can only be seen in the shimmers scattered in the sandy yard. The

years of rain have turned the once shiny roof into a palette of grays and rusty reds. The place seems abandoned, but for the owls and stray cats.

Today, the value is not to the farmer, but to all of us. The function is no longer about what it can hold and keep, but what it can give and teach. There are lessons to learn and stories to tell. There are secrets of a century hidden behind the façade of nostalgic charm. This old barn stoops, but as a muse to artists and a book to the historian, it works still today.

When I stand in the old barn yard and reflect, I can't help but think about myself...

* * *

AGE

EXPOSED!

33

EXPOSED!

Years ago, I used to take many trips by myself. There's a lot to complain about in this fairly rotten world, but the ability for a middle-class country boy to travel is not one of them. I would typically travel to rural locales alone, but after only a handful of trips, I decided I needed to take someone along to verify some of my seemingly unbelievable exploits. Rhonda agreed to be my vérifier (say it with a French accent) and accompany me on my next backwoods trip, as long as I let her drive the rental car, make the important decisions, and pick all of the restaurants. I've given up far more for far less, many times, so I agreed.

After a long jet trip and a couple of hundred miles in a rental car, we settled into a nice cabin on the banks of the Withlacoochee River in central Florida. It was a beautiful rustic place with a dock that was just perfect to sit and watch the river flow by.

After a peaceful evening watching fish jump, birds fly by, and listening to a chorus of frogs, we got up early the next morning for some adventure time. The little cabin came stocked with a long green canoe that seemed perfectly sized for two. Rhonda had never been in a canoe, so the peaceful river was the ideal spot for her inaugural voyage. I assured her it was entirely safe. It was calm. It was shallow. It was 100% gator free.

I admit we had a few awkward moments getting into the canoe, but soon we were gently gliding down the beautiful river. We hugged the bank and maneuvered along, sometimes crouching to squeeze under the branches of tall cypress trees. We saw birds and turtles, and heard splashes and the other sounds of a river alive with wildlife. Since I'm a professional wildlife biologist, I was sure to keep Rhonda full of a nonstop banter of nature facts. I saw in her beautiful face that she was extremely appreciative of my knowledge. Two hours later we were back at the cabin enjoying a sangria in our comfortable chairs on the dock.

That evening I got a phone call from Captain Bob. Captain Bob owns an airboat and gives swamp tours. I had contacted him the previous day, but he only takes his boat out if he has at least five people. He called to tell me that we were in luck, as 3 folks from Scotland were wanting a tour at 4 o'clock the next day. We clinched the deal and would meet him at his dock just down river.

The next day we met Captain Bob and jumped into the front seat of the boat. For the first mile, we idled along through the 5 mph no-wake zone. We passed by the little dock in front of our cabin and continued along the same path that Rhonda and I had traveled in the canoe. It turned out that Captain Bob talked even more than I did, and a lot of his nature talk ran contrary to the fascinating facts that I had dispensed to Rhonda just a day earlier.

Despite his chronic inaccuracies regarding nature, the ride went pretty well, for a few minutes. But things took a turn for the worse when that loud-mouthed Captain Bob told everyone about the hundreds of gators in the area. He pointed and said, "See that big log? I saw a twelve-footer there just yesterday. Bla bla bla bla... I saw a ten-footer over there... bla bla bla..." He just wouldn't shut up about gators.

At this point, I was avoiding any eye contact with Rhonda. But even looking away, I could feel her icy glare. Just the day before, when I had proposed we take the canoe ride, I had guaranteed her that there were no gators in this part of the river. Now, in my defense, I thought that there *probably* weren't any gators in the area, but I made up all kinds of believable sounding reasons why they wouldn't be there. In the process, I cashed in all my clout as a professional wildlife biologist. That babbling Captain Bob was really making me look bad. I finally made eye contact with Rhonda just long enough to give her my eye-rollin' look to let her know that Captain Bob was just spewing some bullshit to scare the three older Scottish folks. I was sure that after a couple of hours in the boat, we wouldn't see a single gator and I could reclaim my authority as a professional wildlife expert.

Captain Bob eased the boat through a little opening between some trees. Rhonda and I had maneuvered the little canoe through the same opening. Well, as often is the case when you're hiding a lie, something big will rear its ugly head, seemingly out of nowhere to expose your secret. In this case, the ugly head was connected to about 200 pounds of Florida alligator and it flopped into the water with a magnificent splash.

It is well known that everyone pays some price for a lie. I'm still paying for mine with a chronic crick in my neck from spending the next 2 hours with my head twisted to the side to avoid eye contact with Rhonda. Gator after gator, I just kept my head turned away. Gator after gator after gator. Eventually, after what seemed like eternity, I couldn't stand the neck pain any longer. I turned for a quick glance at Rhonda. Just as I knew it, she was still staring at me with the look of a woman that was about to throw her lying man overboard, into that "safe" and "gator free" water!

After a few hours, Captain Bob slid the boat back up to the dock and we all got out. Given the nature of this PG-rated story, I'm not at liberty to recount the verbatim details of the one-sided rant that took place in the rental car, the moment the door slammed shut.

"We could have been eaten! They would have never found us! Our kids would be orphans!"

On the drive back, Rhonda was gracious enough to stop by a store so I could grab some Ibuprofen for my neck. Suffice it to say, in all future endeavors, I'll be much more forthcoming about any potential risks associated with our outdoor activities.

Yes, a lie will be exposed, and a liar will face some kind of justice. I know most everyone has some occasional neck pain. But I know that the pain in my neck, even today 10 years later, is my punishment and a continual reminder to be more careful with my facts. To this day, whether I'm in the desert or the mountains or my backyard, if I get a crick in my neck, I can swear I'm seeing gators!

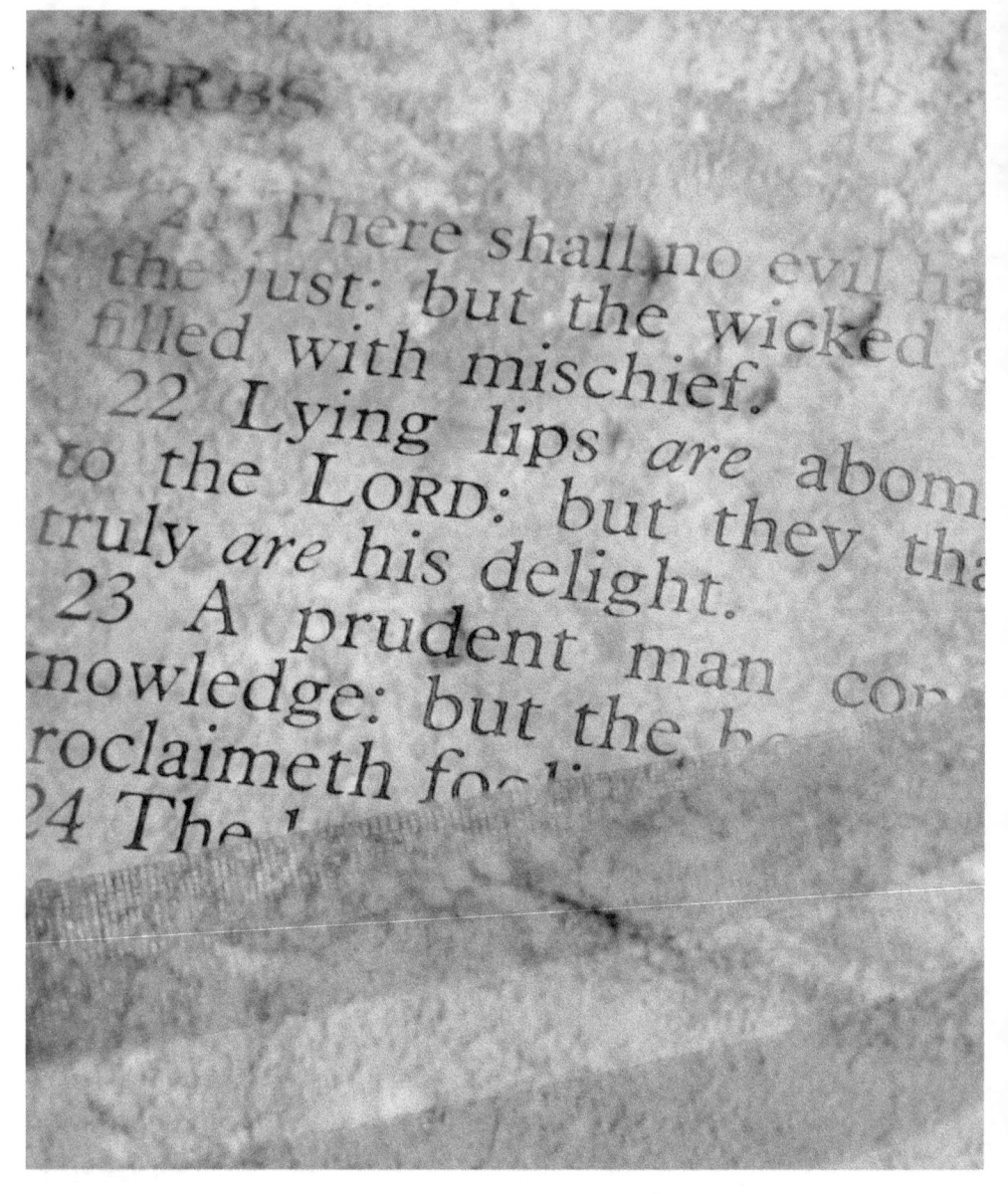

SOMETIMES YOU JUST GOTTA RANT!

34

SOMETIMES YOU JUST GOTTA RANT!

I've always said that somewhere between Zen and crazy is letting out a good rant. It's my time.

As I write, it's only hump day, and I'm already about to jump off the cliff. I am in one of those phases...

"Dear God, please save me... from your people!"

I cringe when I see my Christian friends post something completely untrue and mean on social media. I cringe even more when they get a bunch of "Amens!" and "Hell yeahs!" I see them post links to ridiculous conspiracy theories and mean-spirited memes aimed at anyone on "the other side." Somehow, a zeal for partisan politics has been twisted into doing "God's work."

I've watched as fine Christian ladies post about loving Jesus with all their hearts. I've been sickened when their very next post calls for burying landmines at our border and blowing up those Mexicans trying to get across. They post how they just heard on the news that they're all murderers and rapists and pouring across our border to steal our precious lawn mowing jobs. Then two lines later, claiming those same people are all on welfare.

I see Christian men wearing t-shirts in church, with a cross wrapped in a flag, and big red, white, and blue lettering that reads "God, Guns, and Old Glory!"

We stand in church and sing wonderful old songs that touch my heart. But

I can't help but wonder how long it will be until we start rewriting some of them with an American disclaimer.

*"Jesus loves the little children, all the children of the world." *Some restrictions apply. Subject to Terms and Conditions. American children preferred. Undocumented children specifically omitted.*

We all love the Bible and talk about filling our heads with its words. But then we spend all day filling our heads with talk radio and cable TV news. It seems that the mention in the Bible about being careful who we allow to give us counsel no longer applies.

But I guess I'll get by until Sunday when I can go to church. You know, that building where people walk in during the last worship song and then browse Amazon on their phones during the sermon. When church lets out, we can all go home and get back to the business of blasting and name-calling every person who doesn't fit our mold of a good patriotic American. And maybe next week, we can all sit around in a church committee, scratching our heads and wondering why the pews are getting empty.

All of this makes me a bit sick but does help me recall the first Bible verse that I memorized when I was a kid. It's in the Gospel of John, Chapter 11, verse 35: *Jesus wept.*

As I sat and scrolled through social media, watching so many American Christians taking pride in their offensiveness, I had had enough for a day. I shut everything off, put down my phone, and found a pencil and paper. In sadness, I sat and wrote this poem:

Oh My Soul

Oh my soul, my lovely soul, I'll be leaving you home today. You make it too hard to step over the widows and orphans, the addicted and homeless. You make it just too difficult for me to believe that the poor are all just lazy.

Oh my soul, my weary soul, I'll have to leave you in the car today. You blur my lines and cloud my mind with your notions of love and neighbors and meekness and peace.

Oh my soul, my lonely soul, please wait for me here. I promise I'll be back later. You make it so hard for me to hate all the people that aren't just like me.

Oh my soul, my crying soul, please don't look at me like that. You make me question too many things that I'm told are my American birthright.

Oh my soul, my longing soul, I know...I know... But I'm busy saving the world from them.

Oh my soul, my deserted soul, I don't want us to grow apart. I'll see you at visiting hours on Sunday morning.

Oh my soul, oh my soul.

Well, I don't really feel better. But now it's time to get back to love. As easy as I find it to love the hated, I've got to find a way to show love to the haters, too.

And grace.

Oh Lordy!

* * *

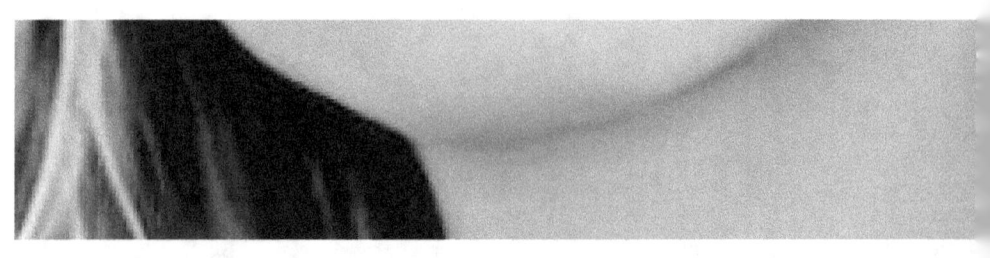

S&M NIGHT

35

S&M NIGHT

Anyone who has been married for more than a few years knows the difficulty of keeping romance alive. A relationship always starts out fun and exciting, but then life comes along to throw the breaks on the passion train. First, it's usually kids, but jobs and the pursuit of money can also send the train completely off the tracks.

Rhonda and I have always put value on romance. It was a struggle while we raised our family, but we managed to find a little time to ourselves. That coveted "us time" was usually after work, and football practice, and dinner, and homework, and the other myriad of daily requirements to keep teenagers happy and growing. Weekend getaways were rare, but we certainly tried to make the best of our situation by lowering some expectations. We spent quite a few nights with a glass of wine in the hot tub well after midnight. A few hours here and a few hours there and we still looked at each other with the dreamy eyes of young lovers. There may have been dark circles under them, but our eyes were dreamy.

Through all that time, well hidden beneath actual words, were the thoughts that raising kids and the hours of busy responsibilities was temporary. Someday, the kids would be grown and self-sufficient and if everything went as planned, they would move out of our house. We wouldn't be those parents complaining about being empty-nesters. Nope. We'd more likely be dancing in the street and wearing "Finally Free" t-shirts.

Almost a decade after the whole world rang in the new millennium and we were getting comfortable writing the date with a 20 rather than a 19, the last of the kids moved out. Hallelujah! We were ready to start living the dream. We'd surely have romantic dinners together every night. We'd get away every weekend and stay in cute little bed and breakfast inns on the coast. We would eat avocado toast every morning, cheer our love with mimosas, and stare into each other's starry eyes. We would talk and plan and pat ourselves on the back for what a great life we had built.

But nothing ever goes as planned. Yes, the kids were gone, but the twelve-hour workdays and seven-day-a-week schedules managed to stay behind. Somehow during the past decade, we had become workaholics and hadn't even noticed. For much of the year, I worked all week and then overtime on Saturdays. Rhonda worked all week, but then led music at church on Sundays. I played guitar on her music team, so our Sundays were always booked. We practiced with the music team on Wednesday evenings, but she and I practiced together at least one other evening. I was the leader of a fourteen-piece gospel band, and we practiced on Thursday evenings. Our concerts were once a month on Saturday nights. Through all of this, we found ourselves with only an occasional evening that wasn't committed to something else. Granted, all of the hustle and packed schedules were important and necessary, but we both knew it couldn't last long without tending to the deeper needs of romance and flirtation and other affairs of the heart.

So, like a zillion other middle-aged couples, we adopted a date night. The concept seemed cliché, but we were desperate. So once every week or two, we would dedicate one evening to just us, and plan a date. We shared the responsibility of planning and would alternate each week. Rhonda would devise a fun evening and the next week I would come up with the evening's activities.

My date nights were pretty basic, consisting of a nice dinner at a restaurant. To prove my romanticism, I'd usually incorporate Uber, so we could have a few glasses of wine. Rhonda would bump it up a few notches when she did the planning. On some of her nights, we'd drive into Old Town Sacramento and spend the night on the Delta King, a 100 year old paddle-wheel river boat that had been transformed into a three-story floating hotel. The beautiful old ship had a bar and restaurant and live music on weekends.

Through the next year or so, we kept to our plan and looked forward to each week's fun. We Ubered to the Studio Movie Grill in Roseville to watch *Fifty Shades of Gray*. We drove into downtown Sacramento for fondue. We visited wineries and antique shops. When we could squeeze in a couple of days, we booked a roomette on the California Zephyr and rode the train over the Sierra mountains to Reno.

One day when we were shopping and running errands in Roseville, we stopped to eat lunch at a small sushi restaurant across the street from a strip mall. While we were enjoying our lunch and talking about how affordable and delicious the sushi was, I noticed a sandwich sign in the parking lot at the entrance. The sign faced the street and had just a couple lines of text:

Couples Special

2 hr massage - $60

I googled it on my phone and the little spa was just three doors down away.

After our lunch, Rhonda walked to the car while I walked over to ask about the couple's special. The windows and doors were tinted, so I couldn't see inside. I was a little apprehensive, but I opened the door and walked in. A string of little bells tied to the door jingled and announced my arrival. I was greeted by a happy lady who was about thirty years old. I asked about the two-hour couple's massage. She started talking loudly and gesturing toward a door that was covered by a curtain. As she tried to escort me into the room, I stammered to try to tell her that I didn't want the massage now and that I was only trying to get information. She offered a few more sentences in her loud voice and parted the curtain. The room was rather dark, but I peeked in. There were two comfortable-looking reclining chairs covered in pillows. The lady continued her barrage of loud talking, but the language barrier was a challenge. She knew very little English, and I knew absolutely zero Chinese. She finally settled into giving me the sales pitch in three-word increments. "One-hour foot here! One-hour body here!" as she pointed to an adjacent room. I told her "Thank you," and she handed me a business card with a telephone number.

I rejoined Rhonda in the car and relayed my best interpretation of what I had seen and heard. We would sit beside each other in comfortable recliners and get foot massages for one hour. Then we would enter a second room and get a full body massage on massage tables. I told her that if we could bridge the language barrier and actually make an appointment, I thought it could be a great date night. We could have sushi for dinner and then walk next door for a massage!

The following week, it was my turn to plan the excitement, so I called the number on the card. The woman who answered had a heavy accent but spoke pretty good English. I told her that I wanted to schedule a special two-hour couple's massage for Thursday at 4 p.m. She told me she could do it at 5 p.m. She took my name and cell number, and it was on the schedule.

On Thursday we arrived at the sushi restaurant at three o'clock. We ordered some edamame, a roll, a beer, and a glass of white wine. Our waitress walked to their counter and passed along our order. I watched as she filled a wine glass from a box in a glass-covered refrigerator. She returned with the wine and an ice-cold beer. The edamame was next, and we finished with a spicy tuna roll. We sat and talked and laughed. We mentioned to the waitress that we were killing some time before our massage, and she was kind enough to tell us we could sit as long as we liked. She kept Rhonda's glass filled and kept me in cold bottles right up to five o'clock.

At the prescribed time, we walked the short distance and stepped into the spa. We were greeted by the manager, NaNa. Her English was good and she told us what to expect during the two-hour session. She led us into the room with the recliners. After we got comfortable, two ladies walked in with buckets of hot water and sat them at our feet. Without a word, they placed our feet into the water and quietly left the room. Rhonda and I lay in the recliners, side by side, eyes closed and let the hot water work on our feet and calves. Before the water cooled, the two women returned and removed our feet and dried them. Within seconds, they disappeared with the buckets of water. Just as quickly, they both returned with short stools and sat down in front of our feet. They put scented lotion onto their hands and started the massage.

It was heavenly! And we were hooked!

After that night, we did it once or twice a month. Sushi and Massage. After a few sessions, I jokingly called it our S&M night—sushi and massage. Even Rhonda got on board… "You ready for an S&M night?" We'd both laugh and I'd respond, "I love our S&M nights!"

I especially liked to call it our S&M nights when someone proposed doing something with us and I'd say, "Oh, I'm sorry. We can't do it on Thursday, that's our S&M night." Then I got to watch Rhonda scramble to tell them how much we love SUSHI and MASSAGE. Yep, SUSHI and MASSAGE. She'd say the words sushi and massage about five times or more to make sure they knew I was talking about sushi and massage. Then she'd give me that look that says, "The moment they leave, I'm gonna kick you right in the ass!"

A perfectly innocent double entendre.

* * *

TREE HUGGER

36

TREE HUGGER

I'm an admitted tree hugger. I celebrate Arbor Day like it's New Year's Eve. I've been involved with the planting of over 50,000 trees. One of the highlights in my life was accepting the Sacramento Tree Foundation's "Tree Hero" award for my work crew. Yes, I like trees. I appreciate them even more now that I have lung issues and need every last molecule of the precious Oxygen that they produce.

I have a long history with trees. When I was a kid, my brother and I watched an old TV movie where a couple of mountain men were sawing down huge trees to build their house. Each time a tree fell, they yelled "Tiiiimmmbbbeeerrr!" It seemed festive and fun, so we walked three miles of dirt roads to the mechanic's shop on our farm and grabbed an antique two-person saw that hung on the wall as decoration. We dragged the eight-foot-long tool back home and were intent on cutting down the only pine tree in the whole area. We managed to get the big saw started into the tree's bark and moved the handles back and forth with all of the strength that four little arms could muster. With every push and pull, we just couldn't wait to yell, "Tiiimmmberrrr" just like we saw on TV. We were about halfway through the tree trunk when my dad rolled up in his pickup truck.

As could be expected, Pops had a fit and laid into us. "Why the hell would you want to cut down a tree?" He grabbed the big saw and threw it angrily into the bed of his truck. After his tirade of foul language and threats of an ass-woopin' if he ever saw us with another saw, he left us with a loud admonishment, "Trees are for planting, not cutting down!"

The tree later died and blew down one night during a storm. We didn't even get to yell TIMBERRR. Dad let it lay there for over a year so I could feel terrible about it every time I walked by.

Even as a kid, I knew I'd have to make up for it somehow, someday. Standing up on the stage to receive the Tree Hero award took a forty-year load off my conscience. Maybe I've paid my penance.

While writing and thinking about my history with trees, I started to realize that we could learn a lot from them. They don't speak much or write books, but they've still got some messages to share.

When I was a teenager, well after the incident with the saw, my dad sent me to do a task on the farm that I felt was way beneath me. It involved cleaning up after an accident with our portable trailer toilet. Use your imagination, and you can probably guess why I felt I was too good for such a messy job. So, I complained and told him how I felt about it.

Pops told me that nothing was beneath me and that we were to do any task necessary, and then do it with the same pride that we'd show in our favorite work. He saw the look on my face in hearing his remarks. You know the look. The ones that teenage boys give their dads when their dads are trying to teach them something that they don't want to hear.

Pops then asked me if I could envision the tall and beautiful trees up in the mountain forests? I said of course I could. I love those trees. He asked me to pick one in my mind and describe it to him. I had no idea where he was headed with his question. So, in my typical smart-assed teenager tone, I described the tree. It was true that I loved the mountain forests and the pine trees, so I described them in such drippy sweet words that it would make a seventeenth century love-struck poet blush. I described the tree's piney smell, its towering height, and the beautiful green of its needles. I went on. I described how the tree looked against the blue sky and then how beautiful it and the others looked when covered in fresh snow. I told him about the whispering sound that the wind made when it blew through the forest. I really poured it on.

When I was done describing that breathtaking tree, Dad nodded and then pointed to a wooden powerline pole about forty feet from us. He said, "That's the same tree, stripped of its beautiful branches and made to stand there naked for years, holding up our stupid high-voltage wires." He pointed again and said, "Look at it, Rawge. It's naked and 500 hundred miles from home, and yet it stands there as tall and strong as it did in the forest." He then told me in his country vocabulary that I need to always seek after the humility of that tree.

So, I guess trees *can* teach us something.

Five years ago, my work staff moved into a brand new building. After pitching the biggest fit, I secured the only corner office. I have two windows and one is directly behind my computer screen. When I look up, I see blue sky and green trees. When I first moved in, there were a pair of Monterey pines that I could see all day. They were tall and wide. Their trunks were thirty feet apart, but the canopies were so big, their tops grew into each other. At the top, it was impossible to tell one tree from the other. On a breezy day, I could watch their limbs mingle and gently touch each other with every sway.

During the first winter in the office, one of the trees blew over during a windy rainstorm. That tree's trunk then lay at a 45-degree angle away from the other tree and their tops no longer touched. It was sad and not the same.

When summer rolled around, the janitor lowered my blinds to keep out the hot afternoon sun. I had another window, facing a different direction, so the blind stayed closed for years and I forgot about the trees.

The other day, the office felt gloomy and I opened the dusty blind to let the light shine in. I sat at my desk and looked out my window. A smile came over my face as I realized that the downed tree had slowly grown one limb back in the direction of the other tree. It had taken five years, but the tree had reached the other tree and they again touched. It had been knocked down, but for half a decade it had quietly put its growth and effort toward its goal, to reach the other tree. The gloom in the office lifted as I again watched the two limbs gently sway and touch, like the outstretched hands of two reunited lovers.

If my dad were here today, I'm sure that he would point to the tree and tell me that I need to seek after the patience and determination and perseverance of *that* tree.

Yes, trees *can* teach us something.

* * *

Roots Gospel Jam
Saturday, Jan 26, 5pm

CLOGGIN'

CLOGGIN' CONTEST
WINNER GETS A TROPHY!

37

CLOGGIN'

"**G**ood evening friends! Welcome to Gospel Jam!" I'd said those words almost a hundred times. It was always at 6 p.m. on a Saturday or Sunday night. The two or three hundred people in the audience would clap and holler in anticipation of a fun evening.

"Tonight, we're gonna have some special fun. We're gonna play some fun old gospel songs – Rhonda's gonna come up and sing a couple of songs with us and just at the end, we're gonna have our annual bubble-wrap clogging contest! Cloggin' man, a little wooden puppet, is gonna come up and give us a cloggin' demonstration and then one of you lucky, and undoubtedly good-lookin' folks, is going to go home with the coveted cloggin' trophy! Our clogging contest and the bubble wrap actually got its origin way back in about 1929. I'll tell you that remarkable story in a while. But now, let's play some music. I'll start out singing, then later in the evening, we'll transition to the good singers!"

I'd grin and glance around the stage at the 14 other musicians and singers.

"Mrs. Trammel you ready?"

From all the way on the other end of the stage, she'd holler "Howwwdeee!" in her best Minnie Pearl voice.

"Alyssa, are you ready?"

Alyssa was shy and would just flash a big smile and wave her hand at me. It was as much to tell me that she didn't want any attention than to signal that she was ready. Next, I'd look over at the seven men on instruments. John on the fiddle and harmonica. Cliff on the dobro. Kenny and two Terrys on guitars. Peter on bass. And Rod on cajon.

"Are any of you actually in tune??"

That would get some laughter from the audience and start to get me excited. But I wasn't there for a little laughter. I was there for the full-on belly laughs. I was there to look out and see the old ladies laughing while holding their hands or scarves over their mouths because they were a little embarrassed at something I said. I couldn't sing very well or play guitar very well. But I could entertain! My gift wasn't musical. I was an entertainer!

Next, I'd look to my other singers on the stage, Mary, Howard and Teresa. Howard was big and loud, but the girls were beautiful and sweet as they could be. I'd look them over and lean into my antique microphone.

"You girls ready?"

Here, the whole audience would bust into laughter at me referring to Howard as a girl. I'd turn back at the audience and the glare of lights and flash my biggest Gospel Jam grin and the show was on!

"OK. Here we go. An old tune in the key of G. *I've Got My Hands on the Gospel Plow*. Sing it with me folks!"

"*Well I've got my hands on the gospel plow and I wouldn't give nothing for my journey now. Keep your hands on that plow, hold on! ...*"

Every song would last five minutes or so and we sang them all with energy. After each song, I'd be about out of breath, so I'd talk a bit, tell a joke or two or tell a story. I would make a big point of telling everyone that every single word that I said was true! True to the best of my imagination. That qualifier got me off the hook a little when I took some liberties to make a story funnier.

We'd usually sing for an hour and a half. Sometimes it would be a hundred degrees in the church sanctuary, but we'd just wipe the sweat off and keep on making music. Sometimes we passed out old-time church fans with our name and logo printed on them. People appreciated them on the hot days, but I never liked that it took one hand away and people would stop clapping to our music. Even worse, it was a little disconcerting to look out past the stage lights and see a hundred fans swaying side to side, and not any two of them on the same beat.

We had done the Gospel Jam for enough years that we fell into a nice pattern that we knew would send everyone home, full and happy. We played music, I told a funny 10-minute true story, we had an audience participation game, and then we ate. And every bit of it was free, we didn't charge for anything. We had a donation can for people who wanted to contribute, but even then, we'd donate the money to a local charity. There were times we sent a few hundred dollars to families that had lost their homes to fires. We gave to animal rescues. We sponsored a small high school scholarship. There was always a need that fell into our radar just before our concerts.

The concerts would be talked about for days after we all went home, but the Roots Gospel Jam Free BBQ Plate Dinner was legendary. The plate consisted of pulled pork sandwich, chips, and homemade coleslaw. People were always amazed that Rhonda cooked all the food, set up the equipment for the concert, ran the soundboard during the concert, came on stage to sing a song or two, and then packed up the whole trailer full of sound equipment at night's end. But no one was more impressed than me.

"Ok friends. Everyone having a fun time?"

No one hid their excitement or sat on their hands. Everyone in the building would clap and holler. That was what made it all worthwhile and everyone on stage felt it. People could cut loose a little at Gospel Jam. Folks could clap and wave their hands. Men could whoop when they felt like it. Kids could run around the building and do stuff that they couldn't do on Sunday morning when it was church. It was that free-spirited fun that got us all in conversations when we were shopping in town. We got stopped coming out of the grocery store. We got stopped coming out of the Indian casino. We got stopped at the post office and we got stopped at the gas station. Lots of fine folks wanted to tell us how much fun they had at Gospel Jam

"It's time for the cloggin' contest. While Rhonda gets the bubble-wrap taped on the floor, I'm gonna tell you a story about my grandpa and how I got the idea to try clogging on some loud bubble wrap."

My Papa Kinley was a figure in my life, even though he died when I was in my early teens. He was tall and thin and kind to a fault. He was a fiddle player and

could fiddle any old folk tune in any key. Unless his hands were busy making a living, they were holding a fiddle. He could repair them with the most basic of tools and could do most anything with just a pocketknife. In the few times that he had five spare dollars, he'd buy a used fiddle, fix it up, and give it to a kid or adult who needed it.

Papa was raised in a very rural part of Arkansas. During winter, he and two brothers trapped minks in the local streams and then sold them at the Sears and Roebuck fur buyer's station. During the rest of the year, they had mules and hired themselves out to plow fields or drag timber. Sometimes they traveled as far away as Missouri to keep their mule teams busy. The brothers were hardworking and industrious. They were poor and life was a struggle. But they did whatever was necessary to keep their families fed and a roof over their heads.

No one saw it coming. First, the Great Depression hit Wall Street like a thief in the night. People went to bed rich and woke up poor. As quickly as the news made rich people poor, the ripples spread across America and made poor people even poorer. As America reeled from the shock, the Dust Bowl rolled into the plains, seemingly just to kick a poor man when he's down. Before the dust even settled, our great country saw lines at soup kitchens and roving men pleading for a day's work and pay. For a large swath of America, the future seemed grim.

For the poor people from town to town, the talk was about California. For the rural poor from hollow to hollow, the talk was about California. Men in Texas found themselves listening to the stories about fields of fruit and vegetables rotting in California, because there were not enough strong men to pick them. These men told their brothers and uncles in Oklahoma. Those men told cousins in Missouri and those men sent word to relatives in Arkansas. Somewhere in the telephone game of stories, my tall Papa cocked his ear and listened.

Even as men sold everything they owned and packed their families into beat up old trucks, Papa was hesitant. Talking to a man who knows a man, who knows a man that received a letter from a relative in California, was not enough evidence. He would need to see it for himself.

Papa started planning. He and his brothers Jeff and Dewey would hop on a freight train and make their way west. Once in California, they could assess the validity of ripe fruit hanging on trees, good wages to pick them, and houses to hold the family.

Much of it seemed too good to be true. California was a half a continent away, but how could it have escaped the dark cloud that seemed to have settled over the rest of the country?

Riding freight trains was not an easy venture. There was no train schedule to guide you. The hobos picked trains based on their cargo. Certain items went east, and other cargo went west. The real vagrants were good at it. But logistics was only part of the problem. If you weren't discovered by a railroad cop and beaten with a club, you could be robbed by other drifters along the way. But Papa and his brothers had some experience. They had rode the rails to Missouri and Oklahoma to work teams of mules and even to Texas to visit relatives. The three brothers were confident that they could cover the 2,000 miles and be back before the Fourth of July. It was mid June.

I don't know the location, or the date, or other details, but I know the story well. Papa told it to me in his Ozark dialect that I learned as a child. He told it to me many times and never refused when I'd ask to hear it again. He used words like kindly when he said "It was kindly hot." He carried his belongings in a satchel and his smaller things in a poke. Papa used the words any more, to mean now: "Any more, I don't put cream in my coffee."

The story began in Dardanelle Arkansas and ended in the same place. In the middle was fifteen-hundred miles of trains and tracks. There were contacts and conversations and nights on hard floors. There were aching stomach-growl hungries, sweat and cold. There was the excitement of seeing the San Joaquin Valley from the Tehachapi mountains. There was lots more. But my story starts on a hot day, in a box-car with an open door, somewhere along the journey.

The three brothers were thrilled to have hopped into a car that had some buckets and crates to sit on. There were two other men in the car, but they sat alone and kept to themselves. Papa and great Uncle Dewey sat on crates and watched the world roll past the door. Uncle Jeff lay in a far corner, asleep on a blanket, with a knapsack for a pillow. What little they had taken along was stuffed into another bag that lay at Uncle Jeff's feet. Everything was stowed, with the exception of Papa's fiddle. It was packed neatly in its little road-worn case and kept within Papa's arm's reach.

It was hot, but the inside of the bouncing boxcar was shaded. It was bright near the open door, but darker towards the corners of the car. Papa took his fiddle out of the case, plucked each string and turned the wooden tuning pegs. He had a master's ear and within a minute, it was tuned. He put it under his chin and drew the bow across a string. It sounded beautiful in the little wooden cathedral. The clickety rails and rumbling floors were a perfect accompaniment, so he started fiddling.

Maybe he played The Arkansas Traveler, a common fiddle tune for the time. Maybe he played The Eighth of January or Sally Goodin'. He knew every reel, jig, and breakdown. He played for over an hour, while Uncle Dewey tapped his toe and smiled. The two strangers in the car dragged their crates closer and listened. Live music was a pleasant reprieve and lively fiddle music could make even the most weary soul feel better.

When Papa finished, he opened his case and carefully laid the fiddle and bow back into their compartments. He covered the violin's delicate strings with a small piece of cloth before closing and latching the lid. Papa nodded at the two strangers and grinned. Each of them grinned back and without saying a word, their smiles conveyed their appreciation. The strangers dragged their seats back to their darker corner of the box car and sat down.

Papa and Dewey talked quietly to each other for a few minutes, when one of the strangers walked back up.

'We'd like to hear some more fiddle music.'

'I don't feel like playing anymore. It's kindly hot. Maybe I'll pull the fiddle out a little later after my fingers rest.'

'I ain't asking, I'm telling.'

Papa looked up to see the stranger holding a little pistol, pointed in his direction.

'Now open it up and get to fiddling, Skinny! Or I'll shoot you both and roll your carcasses off the train.'

Papa looked him over and it was pretty apparent that he meant business. The stranger's appreciative smile was gone and replaced with the kind of look you see on a man's face that has no trouble using a gun to get what he wants.

Papa pulled the fiddle and bow back out of the case and started playing. Fiddling with sore fingers was a small price to pay to keep from getting shot. He played with concentration and avoided looking at the gun barrel just a few feet from his guts.

'Hey fat boy, can you clog?'

'Not much, I'm a little heavy for it.'

'Well get up here and try it. Entertain us, dammit!'

Uncle Dewey got up and stood by the door. His heavy Brogan boots started to shuffle along to the fiddle's tempo. He had watched men clog enough times to know the basic rhythm. He kept his arms hanging while he shuffled his feet. Occasionally he'd stomp a heel to emphasize a beat. It wasn't good cloggin', but it was apparently entertaining. The stranger whooped and applauded to keep Dewey stomping along.

Uncle Dewey was heavy, and before long, sweat was rolling down his face. Papa Kinley could see the toll that the workout was taking on Dewey. He ended his tune, so that Dewey could get a rest.

'Phew! That's about all I can do. I need to sit down.'

The stranger pointed the gun at Dewey's feet.

'Oh no, fat boy! Keep at it! You got a lot whole lot more in ya! Get to cloggin'!'

Papa started another tune and Dewey started cloggin'. Papa played the jig slower than normal, but the stranger sensed that the song was dragging.

'Faster! Come on! Faster!'

Papa jumped the tempo and Dewey tried to keep up. It didn't take along before the sweat was in Dewey's eyes and wet patches were showing on his light shirt. Dewey's heart raced but his feet slowed. By the end of the tune, his feet barely moved.

'I said faster! Faster Goddammit!'

The stranger started firing the pistol into the floor around Dewey's feet. Dewey hopped to avoid the flying bullets and started back into a lively, life or death shuffle. He was cloggin' for his life. The stranger fired two more rounds at the floor, and then everything fell completely silent.

Papa stopped fiddling and Dewey stopped cloggin'. They both looked over to see Uncle Jeff, standing with his hand on the stranger's shoulder and a pistol held firmly against the stranger's head. Papa jumped up and grabbed the other pistol from the stranger's hands.

The strangers hadn't realized that buried in one of Uncle Jeff's knapsacks was an "owl's head" .22 caliber pistol, purchased from the Sears and Roebuck catalog for two dollars. They were so cheaply made, that if you fired six rounds, it'd become too hot to hold. Those cheap guns started the saying, hotter than a two-dollar pistol.

'Damn Jeff! I'm about give out and your brother's about to have a heart attack and you're laying over there sleeping it off! Didn't you hear nothing?'

'I wasn't sleeping it off! I was just kindly tired. I heard all the shooting!'

'Gimme that gun! You're shaking so bad you're liable to shoot his head off!'

Papa got both guns and held one pointed at the two strangers. He made them sit with their legs hanging out of the door,

'Any funny business and I'll kick both of you off! Got it?'

The strangers both nodded. Papa just needed a sane minute to think the situation through. Dewey got a big drink of water from a jug and Uncle Jeff lay back down in his dark spot.

'Ok, It's gonna be like this. There's no way for the five of us to sleep here tonight. One of us would have to stay up all night and keep the gun on you two idiots. So you're just gonna sit there until you see a sandy spot and then jump. If you don't jump soon, I'll kick you both off wherever it might be. I'm doing you both a favor by letting you pick your spot!'

'Look brother, we were just playing. We're sorry for being idiots. If you just let us stay here in the car, we promise we won't cause no trouble,. Please sir. Please.'

'I'm not in the mood to argue. You can pick the spot where you jump, or you can pick a spot for me to shoot you. But make it quick. Start lookin'!'

Papa sat back down onto a crate, but kept the little pistol pointed at the two strangers. He was tired and irritated. He was angry about everything that had happened, but silently glad that the men had shown their true nature in the daylight. Had the men pulled the gun on them in the dark, it could have turned out much worse. He sat and looked at his brother. Dewey leaned back against the wall, still clutching the gallon water jug. Jeff was already asleep, laying on his back with one leg bent at the knee.

Suddenly Papa jumped up.

'We're coming up on a bridge! Stand up and get ready!'

He stepped back a few feet and kicked the stranger's bags in their direction.

'Grab your stuff and get ready.'

Both men were leaning forward to see what was ahead. Papa moved further back in the car to get a better sight angle. The sound inside the car abruptly changed.

They were on a bridge. Papa leaned to see ahead.

'OK, if you can swim, I'd jump in the water. If you can't, then jump when you see some sand! Don't make me kick you out!'

Both strangers frantically pleaded to Papa to let them stay on the train. Papa pointed the barrel of the gun at them and shook his head from side to side.

'Nope, you're getting off. Get ready! Five.... Four... Three... Get ready to jump! Two... ONE!'

At that, both men jumped and a second later, Papa heard a big splash. He looked back to see the men bob to the surface, flailing their arms to grab their packs. As the speeding train got farther away, the last thing he saw was both men dragging themselves up the muddy bank. They were muddy, wet and without a pistol, but they were alive.

"So that's the story folks!"

I leaned into my antique microphone and wiped some sweat from my face.

"That's why some lucky person is going home with the Roots Gospel Jam Bubble Wrap Cloggin' Contest trophy tonight. So contestants, come on up."

While I was telling my story, Rhonda had taped long sheets of bubble wrap on the floor. The eight contestants walked up and took a spot between the stage and the bubble wrap. I nodded to John the fiddle player and he jumped in with a lively old breakdown called Sally Goodin'.

"Ok friends, on the count of five, jump in and start cloggin'! The loudest clogger wins the trophy! Make it so loud that we'll wake up Uncle Jeff sleeping in his grave! I'll say it just like Papa said it."

"Five.... Four... Three... Better get ready to jump! Two... ONE!"

And yes, they were cloggin' and yes it was loud enough to wake up Uncle Jeff.

* * *

INTROSPECTION

38

INTROSPECTION

I've spoken and written many times about the need for daily introspection. My mom summed up Socrates's thoughts that an unexamined life is not worth living, by simply telling me that tomorrow, I'm supposed to be better than I am today.

Mom was smart enough to not offer any details. The curtness of her advice was, of course, the genius in her admonishment. The lack of further direction caused me to have to think. Better at what? Marbles? Math? Reading? Throwing rocks?

Those daily boyhood appraisals have given way to many others and they've slowly gotten a little deeper as I've grown and matured. A better friend? A better husband? A better lover? The list of things that I could be better at could fill a book. A big book!

Once I was walking along a deserted road doing wildlife surveys. Usually, these surveys are in isolated areas, but for this project, I was walking miles of two-lane road shoulders. As I walked slowly along, I used my binoculars to scan for various bird and mammal species. Periodically, I'd stop and listen for a bird's call. The pace was leisurely, and the work was enjoyable.

I had reached an intersection of two small county roads. I pulled a wrinkled piece of paper out of my pocket. I had drawn a line on the route that I needed to take. I glanced up to see the names on the green road signs, turned left, and continued walking. This road had tall weeds on the shoulder, so I would need to walk on the cracked pavement. I rarely saw a car, but an occasional farm tractor would pass by and wave a hello.

All of the roads had random trash scattered along the shoulder. Beer bottles. Fast food cups. I'd seen everything from shoes to cell phones. I always looked down and shook my head at the litter. On this little road, I saw something new, and it made me stop to inspect. A plastic fork.

What many might call the universe or the cosmos, I call God. Either way, I felt that I might be getting a message. Maybe I was being prompted towards some serious introspection when I looked down and literally saw a fork in the road. Granted, there were a couple of spoons and a plastic knife scattered on the road shoulder, but the fork was actually on the road. So, I took it as a sign to do some thinking.

It would have been pretty powerful if I had been facing some big life-changing direction. Should I change my job? Should we buy another house and move? Should I sell my beloved Martin guitar and buy a Gibson? Those are big fork-in-the-road types of questions. But I wasn't facing any of those. So, I looked for smaller, less visible, forks in my road.

When I started looking for those smaller forks, I found that there were many! I doubt there is a single day of our lives that we don't face some kind of little fork in our road or some other "should I" or "shouldn't I" moment. Sure, we might lament and agonize for weeks over the big ones, but I think the myriad of smaller ones are the ones that add up and reveal who we are.

I've come to realize that it is the little ones, the near-momentary decisions that I make each day, that have the biggest effect on my life. Those little ones are the ones I should ponder on each night when I'm finally sitting quietly at home. Yep, those tiny personal decisions are the ones that will determine if tomorrow, I'm better than I was today.

Thanks Momma.

* * *

INTROSPECTION

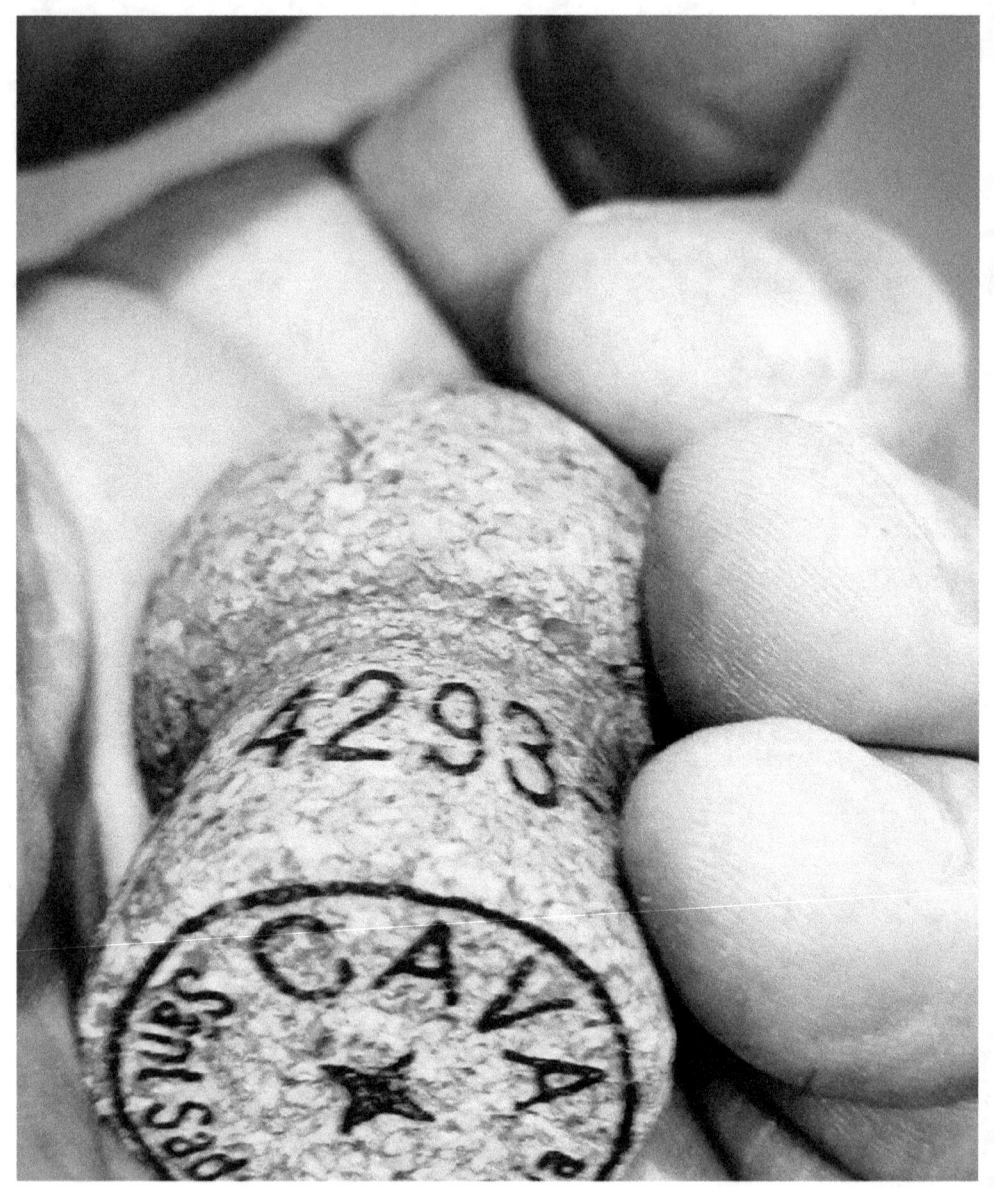

IT'S A MAN'S WORLD

39

IT'S A MAN'S WORLD

Rhonda and I have a nontraditional relationship. Rhonda does a lot of stuff that is more traditionally left to the man. For instance, she does all the driving. I'm a pretty weak driver and I hate driving. She's great at it, be it a country road or the middle of San Francisco. But I see some judgment about this quite often in people's faces. We pull up somewhere with Rhonda driving and I see a man whisper to his wife, "He must have lost his driver's license. I wonder what he did?" Nope. I have a driver's license. We're just nontraditional.

Rhonda also does all of our outdoor grilling. I don't touch the grill except to clean it and keep it full of propane. She's great at it and can grill a steak so tender that you'd wonder how the cow even walked.

A long time ago, my ratty old 300,000-mile Toyota pickup broke down and I got it towed home. Back then when we didn't have two nickels to rub together, getting towed didn't mean calling a tow truck. It meant calling a friend with a tow chain! I got it home and was out in the morning with the hood up. As I stared at the engine, Rhonda came walking out. In her cute little voice, she asked, "What's wrong with it?" I said I didn't know, but I was working to figure it out. So, she asked questions.

Her: Did it just up and die? Me: Yes. Her: Did you take the breather off and pump the throttle to see if it's getting gas? Me: Yes, I've already done that. Her: OK, did you remove a spark plug wire and crank it to see if it's getting spark? Me: Yes, I did that too. Her: Does it crank and pop every once in a while? Me: Yes. Her: Then I bet it's a cracked distributor cap.

At that point she was just getting on my nerves. So, in a very manly voice, I told her that I wouldn't tell her how to handle the kitchen and she's not to tell me how to handle the vehicles. She said, "Fine!" and headed back for the house.

About an hour later, Rhonda came back out to find me standing in the same place. She asked if I was having any luck. I said no. She responded in her cute Southern voice, "Come on, let's go down to Napa and get a distributor cap. Don't worry... I'll drive."

An hour later the truck started like it was new. That's when I learned that Rhonda had spent a big part of her childhood working in her dad's parts store in Alabama.

But not long ago, I realized there's one area around here where it's still a man's world.

When Rhonda peels the foil and wire twists off the top of an old bottle of nice champagne and the cork won't even wiggle, it gets handed straight to me!!! I have perfected a way to grasp the cork that manages to bulge every last muscle I've got, and then POP!

And for that brief moment, it's a man's world, Baby!!!!

* * *

IT'S A MAN'S WORLD

MY FRIEND, THE MEAN BRAIN

40

MY FRIEND, THE MEAN BRAIN

I don't really understand how the brain does its work. I certainly don't understand how mine sometimes works against me. I mean, we should be buds. We're on the same team. We should have common goals. We should just get along.

I have to admit, most of the time we're good. But sometimes, there's a part of my brain that just tries to make my life more difficult. I've heard it said that there are two sides to every brain and I believe it.

Here's an example. When I'm playing music in front of people, be it a concert or in church, one half of my brain buckles down to do its job. I watch my chord sheets and change chords at the proper beat. I read the lyrics and sing when I'm supposed to. I feel the music and create dynamics. I watch Rhonda for any cues that we're about to change something. My mind is pretty busy, but we do our job.

But almost every time, there's the other half of my brain that just messes with me. This part of the brain apparently thinks it's funny to see what it can do to rock my concentration. During a song, it will invariably say something to me like, "Look over there. That nice lady Sharon is staring at you. She's mad. This is her favorite song and you're butchering it!" Sure enough, when I look over, I'll see the nice lady looking at me. Then I can't think of anything else. I just want to get through the song, so maybe I can do better on the next one.

Sometimes it gets even worse. I'll be playing and feeling pretty good about the song, but my mean-brain starts in again. It'll say something like, "Feel that air down there? Your zipper is down!" Well sure enough, if I think about it, I'll feel some breeze down there. Then it just gets worse. It's not like I could look down over my guitar to check it out and prove mean-brain wrong. Nope. All I can do is just try to shut it out and hide the embarrassment of the possibility that I'm a grown man playing music in front of people with his zipper down! By the time the song is over, I'm afraid to even look down because by then, mean-brain has probably convinced me that I don't even have pants on!

So lately, I've been trying to spend some time to get to know that part of my brain. I just want us to be friends. I want us to work together. I want us to do great things and be proud of them. I want us to be a team!

I've come to realize that as much as that part of my brain annoys me, it's that feral and free part of my brain that keeps me young. It's that part of my brain that says stop being an old man and smack your woman on the booty at an inappropriate moment. It's that part of the brain that keeps the fun going.

So we've been hanging out, talking and spending some quality time. I promised to quit calling him mean-brain and just call him M.B. He likes that. He laughs and says it actually stands for More Balls.

Next week I've got some fun trust-building exercises planned for me and M.B. So if you see me walking around and seemingly talking to myself, you'll know what's up. Just smile and say, good morning! Nice to see you two!

* * *

MY FRIEND, THE MEAN BRAIN

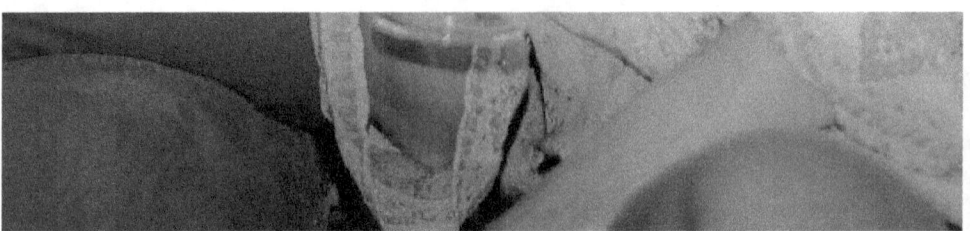

BOUGEE

41

BOUGEE

B ougee. Rhonda and I love to throw that word around a lot, for fun. It means "Aspiring to be a higher class than one is. Derived from bourgeois." Champagne in a nice ice bucket is bougee. A six pack of beer in a styrofoam cooler, well, not as much.

Once when Rhonda and I were in Cabo San Lucas, we managed to get last-minute reservations at a five-star Italian restaurant. For 30 years, Rhonda has been coaching me and helping me along for these occasions. We dressed up in our nicest clothes. Rhonda looked stunning and even convinced me that I'd cleaned up well. We looked bougee.

We arrived at the restaurant early and I had a nice conversation with the maître d'. We spoke mostly in Spanish. The topics meandered through geopolitics, pop culture, music and ended with a discussion on the Mexico and USA relationship. I did well. We got seated at one of the nicer tables in the restaurant.

The waiter spoke some English. We discussed what we had planned to order and then spent several minutes on the wine list, picking a perfect pairing. I did well again. I can finally speak the language!

During the meal, I chose the correct spoons and forks for each course. As our wine glasses emptied, the waiter would carefully refill them, ending the pour with a perfect twist of the bottle. Rhonda and I slowly ate our meal while we chatted and stared into each other's eyes. The entire evening was the pinnacle of bougee-ness.

We sat and sipped our wine. We smiled at the other couples around us, and they smiled back. We listened as the soft and romantic music played just below our voices. Everything was beautiful. But in the final minutes of our romantic evening, I guess I needed to remind the world that you can take the boy off the farm, but you can never take the farm off the boy.

For the last pour from the wine bottle, I just couldn't resist grabbing it and pulling the cork out with my teeth for a loud thuunnkk and yelling ARRRGGGG, pirate style!

We didn't talk much on the walk back to our hotel. I'm sure it'll all be forgotten someday, and I'll get another chance. But just in case, can anyone recommend a good marriage counselor? Asking for a friend.

* * *

PERFECT TIMING

42

PERFECT TIMING

I 've really learned that as you get older, it is easy to look back on your life's timeline and see things that were invisible at the time. I look back through 60+ years of memorable events, people, places, and situations, and realize that so much of it was just a matter of timing.

A good example is the fluctuating price of oil. As I write this, crude oil is about $100 per barrel. In 1986, the price fell from $30 a barrel to only $10 a barrel. That drastic drop would be just an historic blip for most people. But for me and many others working in the Coalinga, California, oil fields, it was life changing. We all worked ten or more hours every day, keeping the precious light-sweet crude flowing from our little town's 1600 oil wells. We did it in the wet and muddy winters and we did it in the hot and dry summers. The only thing that ever changed was the clothes that we wore.

Before the year closed, we opened the newspaper to the fearful news of the Chernobyl nuclear reactor meltdown and the heartbreaking news of the Space Shuttle Challenger explosion. That was front-page news. But for many of us on the west side of the San Joaquin Valley, reading about the oil price collapse, in the back pages of the paper, was just as devastating. It was smaller news to the world, but for a whole community of men and women who wore greasy hardhats and leather gloves every day, they were difficult words to read.

I and many others found ourselves trying to transition from working every day to suddenly struggling just to get enough work to keep the bills paid. That oil-patch money kept the lights on and food on the table. A whole bunch of us were suddenly introduced to something totally new – sitting at home and hoping that the unemployment check would pay the rent.

One day I walked out to our mailbox and grabbed the mail. There was no check, but mixed in with the assorted bills was a newspaper-sized flyer for our local community college. I had seen it many times and it was always addressed to a guy named "Boxholder." Colleges, even a little junior college, didn't send invitations to Roger Jones.

I was bored, so I browsed through the classes that were being offered. I had never been much of a student, but every time I got one of these flyers, I would entertain the notion of taking a class. This time though, I thought about it quite a bit and wondered what it would be like to try a college class almost six years after I left high school.

In a brave moment, I called their number and asked if I could come in and speak with a counselor. A friendly woman on the phone told me, "Of course," and set up an appointment for the following day. The next day, I cleaned up and made the twelve-mile drive into town. I checked in at the office and before I could even sit down, a lady came out to introduce herself. I sat, nervously, in a chair facing her desk and explained my situation. She seemed to know exactly where I was in life. I told her that given my new spare time, I was considering signing up for a class. She asked why I wouldn't sign up for four classes and become a full-time student? She impressed on me that I was currently jobless. She described grants and other financial sources that might be available to me. She explained that anything I was lacking from my high school record could be made up during my coursework. She assured me that there were tutors available if I had problems. She was good. It wasn't exactly the pressure of a timeshare sales pitch, but after some discussion, I was enrolled in four classes. I walked out of the office a little shocked. One day I was a backhoe operator in the oil fields and the next day I was a 26-year-old, full-time college student.

Two years later I graduated from the community college with near perfect grades and two years after that, I graduated from the University of California, Davis. Somewhere in there, oil thankfully regained its price, and the oil fields went back to work. I guess I didn't notice with my face buried in math, English, biology, and history books.

It's all about timing.

In May 1990, 200 million people in 141 countries celebrated the first Global Earth Day. Part of that 200 million people were the Sacramento office of the National Audubon Society and some volunteers. This dedicated group planted 1800 little oak, cottonwood, and willow trees in an area of land, just outside of Elk Grove, California. At the time, I'm sure that I thought "Good for you, tree huggers." I'll be banging on drums and dancing with hippies in the UCD quad. Well, I didn't plant the trees, but I was more than happy to take advantage of Earth Day when the Audubon group advertised to hire a student intern to take care of all those trees. That student job eventually turned into my current job that I'm about to retire from, more than 30 years later. I'm life-long friends with many of those Audubon people. And I'm a tree hugger.

It's all about timing.

I could go on and on. It was perfect timing when I met Rhonda, the love of my life. It was perfect timing when we managed to buy a house 25 years ago, at the very bottom of the housing market. I could go on and on.

The thing about all of this is that it was basically just dumb farm boy luck. Forty years ago, I didn't look at job data and oil price forecasts and then make an informed decision to take advantage of the situation and enroll in college. Twenty-five years ago, I didn't investigate housing price trends and jump in to take advantage of a predicted bull market. Nope, I mostly just stumbled through life and got lucky here and there. You probably have too.

So, I guess that as I sit here under a palm thatch palapa, with waves splashing at my feet, my writing tablet on the table beside my tequila sunrise, I'm just wondering how life might unfold if we could somehow be better at seeing those "perfect time" situations while we are in them. What if we saw them in real time, rather than just an old man looking back through his years of life? What if we saw them and owned them, big and small? I bet a bunch of folks could look around and see that right now there's three jobs available for every one candidate. Someday we could look back and see that data. But we're in it today. Right now might be the perfect time to ask for a raise or even change jobs. Someday we might look back and see data on the affordability of community colleges and the amount of aid available. But it's available today. Right now might be the perfect time to get back in school.

There's always more. Someday we might look back and remember when someone we love was still with us. Right now might be the perfect time to tell someone that you love them. Twenty years from now we might be looking back and seeing a time before something went terribly wrong. Right now might be the perfect time to decide to stop doing something that we know we shouldn't. Someday we may look back and see that today we're following the wrong people, and heading down a dangerous path. Today might be the perfect time to change directions.

You may be reading this story 20 years from now, in a dog-eared copy of this book that you found in a thrift store. It doesn't matter. Let's all look around. Right now is the perfect time for something!

* * *

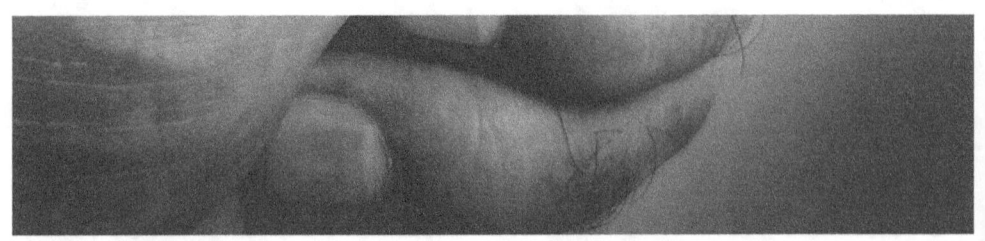

I'M 100% SURE!

43

I'M 100% SURE

I had a conversation with a friend a few days ago. During our talk, we were discussing some work I'm planning to do on our house that involved some wiring. He told me that a mutual friend we've known for years was working on his house and got electrocuted. I said, "Oh no! That's horrible. I hadn't heard about it! I should probably call his wife."

My friend had a puzzled look on his face and then told me she's fine and that our friend was fine. I said, "Well ok, then he got shocked, not electrocuted." My friend said, "Whatever. They're both the same." I told him they were not the same and that shocked means he tangled with electricity, but that electrocuted means he tangled with it, and lost. Yep, it means he died. My friend again wrinkled his nose and told me I was all messed up and that they mean the same thing!

So, I played with him for a minute. I asked if he was sure about his words. He said "Yes."

I asked if he'd bet on it. "Yes."

I asked if he'd bet $50. "Yes."

$100? "Yes."

His life? "Yeah... probably."

So, I asked him to pull his phone out and look it up. He grabbed his phone and started talking to it, like us old people do, and asked for the definitions.

I watched his face as he read the results. He stared at the phone for a minute, scrolled it with his finger, and then said, "Well shit!" He looked back up at me, shaking his head.

I just laughed it off and told him the old adage that we learn something new every day. I was ready to move on in the conversation. But he wasn't. He just stood there looking at his phone. After about a minute, he looked squarely in my eyes and asked, "I wonder what the hell else I'm 100% sure of and I'm 100% wrong about?"

We eventually moved on and talked about other stuff, but I realized that my friend's question to himself is 100% a good question for all of us. How much of what we steadfastly believe to be true is, in fact, not true? How much of what we believe and think has been built by hearing it 50 times on TV news, or Facebook, or some guy we watch on YouTube. We hear something over and over but it's just not true or correct. Maybe it's as simple as just being wrong on the meaning of a word. Or maybe it's something bigger, like concepts, or views, or what we think about others. In today's world of information, I wonder how much of what we get is truth and not slanted opinion? We need to be careful. We'll probably never need to bet our lives on anything, but our reputations are always on the line.

This silly "shocking" conversation with my friend probably changed his thinking a little. He might never say he's 100% sure of anything again. He might now say that he's 90% sure about being 100% sure.

Anyway, it's something to think about. How sure are we? But I'll think about it later. I've got some Facebook to scroll and some news to watch. And I just heard about a guy on YouTube who has all the answers and he's 100% right, 100% of the time.

Gotta go!

* * *

I'M 100% SURE

THE PANDEMIC

44

THE PANDEMIC

I t was March 2020 and my birthday fell on a Tuesday. There was no party, but that evening my wife Rhonda and I sat on our front yard patio and opened a bottle of champagne. To look around and listen, everything seemed normal. Cars still drove by on the road out front. Birds still sang in the trees hanging over our yard. I could still hear our rural neighbors in the distance. Everything seemed the same as any other March day.

But nothing was the same. The week before, my employer had required that I work from home as much as possible. There were days that I didn't wake up in the morning at 5 a.m. and make the 30-minute drive to the wildlife refuge as I had for over 30 years. Three days that week, I sat at our kitchen bar and worked on my laptop computer for nine hours. After work, I sat on the couch and listened to the news. There was a new virus spreading around the world, and we knew nothing about it. We heard reports that it had come from China and many people were dying. We heard that hospitals in Italy were full of dying people and had dead bodies stored in refrigerated trucks. We heard new words, like isolation and quarantine. We used our phones to look up words like ventilator and comorbidity and antibodies. Nope, nothing was the same anymore.

Each evening, our president would go on the news and tell people not to worry. Whatever we were seeing and hearing about other countries would never happen here. As our government began tracking the number of cases, the president would tell us each evening that the numbers didn't mean anything, or that they were wrong. He assured us that the disease would soon just disappear. He had no plan and gave absolutely no reasoning behind any of his assurances. While the rest of the world braced and planned for a battle with an invisible enemy, we would rely on not much more than arrogant American exceptionalism. It will never happen here.

As Rhonda and I sipped my birthday champagne and ate charcuterie, I studied a tree limb that grew across our patio and hung over the roof of our house. I had looked at it many times and noted in my mind that I should cut it down. Winds were predicted the following week, and I didn't want it falling on the house. With all of the worry in my world, I could reduce one piece of it with a day's work. It would be a tough job, but at 60 years old, I was still strong and able.

Saturday morning found me sipping coffee and staring up at an 18-inch diameter limb that spanned 30 feet. Most of it was about 15-feet high and at least 10 feet of it was above our roof. I studied its angle from various points in the yard. It would be an easy job for a tree professional, but Rhonda and I don't hire professionals. We are do-it-yourselfers. During our 25 years in the house, we had remodeled every room from floor to ceiling. We had just finished removing an entire wall that separated the kitchen from the living room. We finished the job and were rewarded with an open kitchen, dining room, and living room. The wall was gone and the house hadn't collapsed, so surely we could cut a large limb down without it crashing through the roof.

I assembled a pile of tools in the front yard. A gas-powered chainsaw, some rope, and a pole saw with a 16-foot handle. I dragged my 12-foot ladder into place, and I was ready to start. It was a good arm workout, but I cut the smaller limbs with the pole saw and let those lighter pieces fall onto the roof. Soon I had the long limb, bare and visible. I broke every safety law and climbed the ladder to the top, tied a rope to the end of the limb, and dropped the rest of it to the ground. I would saw through the limb, and Rhonda would pull the falling limb away from the house and away from the ladder's feet. It would be a tough pull, but Rhonda was as strong as she was pretty.

As I cut through the limb with the chainsaw, I heard the crack of the last bit of wood, even above the saw's roaring engine. I leaned back all I could and watched the whole thing swing and crash onto the lawn. It had missed the roof by mere inches, but in this case, an inch was all that mattered. We patted ourselves on the back for a while and bragged about how perfectly we had planned the complicated event. In less than an hour, I had the remaining limb sawed into 6-foot-long pieces and lying in the yard. One by one, I hoisted each 200-pound piece onto my shoulder and carried it the hundred yards to a pile on the back of our 1-acre property. The whole mess was done and cleaned up by noon.

The next morning, it was my day to go into work. I woke up feeling a little sick. I had a minor cough and my body hurt all over. I knew it was surely just the way that life pays you back for overdoing it. A 60-year-old man shouldn't be trying to do the physical work of a 30-year-old. I drove to my office, worked 9 hours without seeing a soul, and then drove home.

I walked through the door and told Rhonda that I didn't feel good. We took my temperature, and I had a mild fever. I spent the rest of the day in bed and felt confident that I'd be better by morning. A good night's sleep can cure anything.

I didn't get a good night's sleep. My fever got worse, and I had trouble breathing. When I wasn't coughing, I was struggling just to breathe. Rhonda pleaded with me to let her take me to the emergency room. I still felt that it was something that would pass, but to please her, I scheduled a phone call with my doctor. Neither of us dared to say the word Covid-19. I put that thought out of my mind, even as I lay in bed, drenched in sweat, eyes closed, but listening to the president's evening message on TV. He said it was not affecting the USA much because he'd done such a great job in preventing it. He bragged about how much testing that our country was doing and then bragged about how many tests were on hand for our hospitals and doctors. He ended by saying that anyone that wants a test can get a test. That was the only part of his message that was comforting. If it came to it, I could at least get a test and know what I'm dealing with.

By noon the next day, I could hardly talk. It took all my dwindling strength just to get out of bed and walk the few steps to the bathroom. At exactly 1 p.m.,

I received my doctor's call on my cell phone. I didn't have enough strength to hold the phone, so I propped it on a pillow. My doctor asked me questions and I struggled for enough breath to answer her. What was my temperature? How difficult was it to breathe? How was my strength? Did I have pains? We talked for about 5 minutes. She ended the call with the words that I had dreaded, "Mr. Jones, it sounds like you have Covid-19." She would request a test from the CDC and call me back. While I waited, I was to get myself ready to make the drive to the testing location.

Rhonda stood in the doorway during the call. She was already doing her best to care for me, while trying to stay out of the room as much as possible. Even if it wasn't Covid, it was still possibly something that was contagious. But at hearing the doctor's news, everything got scarier. She looked at me and said, "Good. Let's get the test and maybe they can do something for you." She got some clothes for me and laid them on the bed. As soon as the doctor called back, she would help me to the car and drive me to the testing location.

After about 15 minutes, the doctor called back. She went straight to the news. "Mr. Jones, the CDC denied your request for a test. There's only a limited number of tests. You can only get a test if you've been in close contact with a confirmed Covid case." I argued with her that there were plenty of tests. I had just heard it, straight from the president's big mouth, that we've got millions of tests and that if I wanted a test, then I could get one. She countered that I could take that up with the president, but the CDC said no. She followed with the assessment that she was sure I had it and that there is no cure. If I went to the emergency room, I would only be putting others at risk. There was nothing they could do. I was to stay at home, rest, and try to get better. I interpreted her words to mean that I was to stay at home, rest, and try not to die. She would call me back the next day.

My hopes were gone. This wasn't just the result of an old man playing Paul Bunyan for the weekend. I was sick, and possibly with a disease that was killing people. I was afraid. How did this happen to me? Had I infected Rhonda during the past two days? Would I just die in my sleep? How long would it take? A day? Two days? I lay in the bed, worried for myself and Rhonda. I worried that she was just a day or two behind me. I lay there angry. Who had infected me?

Were they OK? Did I spread something to my work? Why did the president lie to us?

I struggled through another night. The next day, I called my doctor back. I told her that I wasn't going to just lie down and try not to die. I wanted a doctor to look at me. If I did die, I wanted it to be after someone looked me over and sent me back home. I insisted that I was determined to go to a hospital. After some arguing, the doctor made me an appointment at a walk-up center for potential Covid-19 cases. I was to go there the next day at 4 p.m., walk up alone and wearing a face covering. I said thank you and hung up.

My condition worsened through the night. My temperature was slowly going up. I hadn't eaten for two days, but Rhonda kept me drinking water. She brought me wet towels for my face and tried her best to be positive. Each time I opened my eyes in the dark room, I could see her silhouette standing in the doorway, watching over me. I prayed and she prayed. Soon it would be daylight.

The next morning, I called my doctor again. I told her that if I had to wait until 4 pm, I wouldn't be able to walk out to the car. It was now or never. She put me on hold and left the line. She returned to tell me that I could go to the walk-up at 10:30 am.

I couldn't stand long enough to take a shower, so Rhonda brought me a wet towel. I washed my face, hands and arms and got myself dressed. I walked into the living room and sat down. It was time to go.

We got to the walk-up area a little early. A lady wearing scrubs and a surgical mask approached the car and asked my name. She told Rhonda to stay in the car and for me to follow her. I shuffled my feet to follow her and we disappeared behind the walls of a tent, set up in the parking lot. I answered a few questions and was handed a plastic bucket. A nurse attached an instrument to my finger and dropped the rest of it into the bucket. I was told to walk to the end of the tent and back. After only a few steps, I felt hot and dizzy and was struggling to breath. The nurse came and steadied me and looked at the instrument in the bucket. She made some hand gestures to the other nurses at the station. They exchanged some words, and I was led into the ground floor of the adjoining building.

The room was large but had been portioned into some makeshift cubicles, separated by plexiglass walls. Each had a single chair in the middle. The nurse helped me sit down and told me someone would be right back to talk to me. Suddenly I was separated from Rhonda, in a strange place and not knowing what would happen next. I prayed and waited. I was afraid. I pondered trying to get up and make my way back to Rhonda. I'd just take my chances at home with her. We are partners through everything. But before I could stand, a nurse appeared at the cubicle. "Mr. Jones, your oxygen level is extremely low, and your temperature is 102.8. We need to get you to a hospital. Just sit here and relax. An ambulance will be here right away."

I got my phone out of my pocket and texted Rhonda. "They are taking me to a hospital. I'm scared."

I had hardly finished typing when two men rolled up with a gurney. They got me into it and rolled me to an ambulance waiting outside. As they were lifting it up, Rhonda ran up to the ambulance and handed me a phone charger. I could see her beautiful eyes and worried face as they closed the doors. The EMT put a mask on my face and started giving me oxygen. I asked where they were taking me. He said the name of a hospital that I didn't recognize. I asked if there was any way that they could take me to Roseville. That was the only hospital that I was familiar with. He responded with a curt, "No sir, you might not make it to Roseville." I closed my eyes. The paramedic took my blood pressure and checked my heart. I lay with my eyes closed, thinking of Rhonda doing her best to follow the ambulance. I prayed. I prayed that she wouldn't be sick next.

The drive to the hospital was only a few minutes, but my condition went down hill quickly. Things got so bad, so quick, that I have only one memory of being in the ER. I recall some nurses trying to help me to lie on my stomach, in hopes that my breathing efficiency would be improved. It didn't help, and in fact, it made it worse. Soon, Rhonda got a call that I was being intubated and placed on a ventilator. She was told that the situation was very grim and to settle in for a long process. Covid restrictions did not allow her in the hospital. She could not be by my side. She could not hold my hand. The nurse assured her that they would call her regularly with my progress. Rhonda cried. She prayed. And she went to Facebook to ask others to pray. The results were immediate. Her post was shared and shared and shared and people around the country and the world joined her in prayer.

A ventilator is a last resort. None of us have ever seen the sight of a grown man, starving for oxygen. If we could see it, we'd better understand the decision. It was described to me that every muscle in my chest was heaving up and down to try to get enough oxygen into my body. It's the body's survival response. But it soon becomes so exertive, that the big chest and back muscles are working so hard and using more oxygen than what is being produced. Shortly after that, you will die.

I was given two powerful drugs through an IV. One of them put me into a deep coma. The second drug paralyzed me. A tube was put in my mouth, down my windpipe, into my lungs. The ventilator supplied me with pure oxygen and did my breathing for me. This last resort would keep me alive for some amount of time. I could lie on the bed, in deep sleep, and allow my doctors a little more time to try to fix whatever was wrong.

When I first rolled into the hospital ER, I was immediately given a Covid-19 test. It came back negative. A little later, I was given a second test, which also came back negative. Two negative Covid tests started a race to find out what was trying to kill me, before it won.

I believe that all doctors are good, but I was fortunate to have a team of doctors that were great, and they went to work. Rhonda had many telephone calls with each of them. Dr. Patel, Dr. Capule, Dr. D'Cruz, and Dr. Glen all had questions for Rhonda. What had I done prior to my sickness? The tree I had cut down became important. Where had we traveled? Our recent trip to Panama became important. What had I done at work the preceding weeks? My coworkers gave Rhonda a list of things I had done during the past two weeks as a wildlife biologist. That news brought in a whole new slew of possibilities. The doctors tried test after test. If they could pinpoint the disease, then they could possibly target it with a specific antibiotic or treatment. But test after test came back negative or not helpful. Soon there were hundreds of disappointing results and no definitive answers.

As I lay in my coma, Rhonda could not be by my side. But she couldn't sit at home either, so each day, she would drive to the hospital parking lot, to at least be closer. She would stand outside her car and look at a window that she had decided was my room. She knew it might be a janitor's closet, but as far as she was concerned, it was my room. She posted about her time in the parking lot and vowed to be there each day. The next day there were other people there. She saw both of our children there, in separate cars, but close enough to talk with each other. She saw friends and others. Soon there were people leaving signs, pointed towards the windows.

WE LOVE YOU RAWGE!

GET WELL RAWGE

GOD BLESS HEALTH CARE WORKERS

As I still lay in a coma, I was being tested for anything that had any potential for my condition. I was tested for things that I cannot even pronounce. But each test came back negative ...*Coxiella burnetii, Staphylococcus aureus, Legionella pneumophila, Pneumocystis jirovecii.* All negative. *Urine microscopy, Mycoplasma pneumonia, Erythrocyte sedimentation rate, Pneumocystis pneumonia, Hypersensitivity Pneumonitis.* The list goes on, and on, and on.

Each evening, Rhonda would post an update on Facebook. Her updates would be shared by friends. There were whole families praying. There were groups praying. There were whole churches praying. There were people praying in other languages. There were people praying who had never prayed before. All of them were worried and monitored Facebook for Rhonda's updates.

A few nights into my induced coma, Rhonda sat in bed. She was alone, worried and crying. Between tears, she prayed. Between more tears, she looked at pictures on her phone and thought about our memories. Each picture brought happy thoughts. Pictures of us with the kids and grand-kids. Our trips throughout the world. Us dressed up and in happy places.

At midnight, as she still sat in bed, her phone pinged that she had received a text. Even with the late hour, it wasn't too startling. She had received many texts from many friends in other time zones. When she looked at her phone, this one *was* startling–it was a text from me!

The text was simple. "I love you baby! I'll see you when I wake up well *Rawge*"

Rhonda stared at the text. How could this be? That is impossible. I was in an induced coma and induced paralysis. My phone, wherever it was stored, had a pin lock on it. Texting from it would have been impossible. And yet, there it was. Through tears, she read the text over and over. She wondered if she was dreaming. Was she asleep and it wasn't even real?

Shortly after, as she sat in bed, with the phone clenched to her chest, it rang. Someone was calling. She glanced at the screen. It was a call from me. She pushed the green button and spoke into the phone.

Rawge? Is it you? Are you there?

She could hear muffled beeps and blips and the other sounds that you would expect to hear in a hospital room with a patient on life support systems.

She asked again, Rawge, is it you? The response was taps on the phone. *Tap tap tap. Tap tap tap.* Whether it was me or not, she started talking. She told me that she loved me. She told me that she missed me. She told me that people all over were praying. She prayed into the phone. She talked about all the things we would do when I got home. She talked about anything that popped into her head.

Occasionally she would pause and ask, Rawge, are you still there? Each time, her question would be answered by taps on the phone. *Tap tap tap. Tap tap tap.* The call lasted for over 3 hours, and then the line went silent and disconnected.

As anyone would expect, the night's events had given her a strong sense of wonder, but also a strong sense of hope. Whatever it was, however it happened, it had brought some peace. She and I had joked many times about our "Radar Love," each time we both texted "I Love You" at the same time, or we both called each other at the same time. This was somehow that. But it was something that she wouldn't tell anyone or talk about for months.

The next morning, as the nurse was leaving her shift, she called Rhonda to tell her that I had a good night. I wasn't any better, but there had been no issues. Rhonda asked her to check my bed to see if I had a phone. She chuckled that of course I didn't have a phone, but that she would check. She reported back, astonished, that there was a phone on my chest, with a dead battery. Rhonda said thank you, and asked if she would please leave it somewhere close.

Three days after that night, Rhonda got a call from Dr. Glen with the great news that I was being removed from the ventilator. The steroids and general antibiotic drugs that I had been receiving were working. I was at a point that she felt my body could breathe on its own, with oxygen administered through my nose. It was a glorious day!

I would still spend another week in the ICU and a couple more weeks in the hospital. It was days before I had enough energy to sit up in bed and even more days before I could stand. I had many *two steps forward, one step back* days. I would be moved to a regular hospital room, only to be taken back to the ICU the next day.

One morning, my heart went a little crazy and I had to have an emergency cardioversion. That's a long word that means that they gave me a drug that stopped my heart from beating, in hopes that when it restarted, it would be in a normal pattern. For several seconds, I lay in the bed attached to electrical wires, but with no heartbeat. A nurse held my hand and we all watched a screen, hoping for the familiar little green blip to reappear. It did and it was normal. There were other scares, but slowly I got better.

After over a month in the hospital, I was allowed to go home. I would say goodbye to all of the nurses and doctors that had taken such loving care of me. I would miss Grace or Pat waking me in the middle of the night to draw more blood into the little vials. I'd miss Lana taking her breaks to sit and talk with me. I'd miss Maribeth and Gill, bringing my pills and cheerfully telling me that I'd be ok. There were many others that cared for me, and unfortunately there'd be an unending supply of sick people that needed my bed and their care. It was time to go home.

My doctors arranged for an oxygen generator to be delivered to our house. I couldn't walk more than a few steps and would require supplemental oxygen 24 hours a day, but I could see Rhonda!

That first hug and kiss will be in my memory forever. It took weeks before I could walk much more than to the bathroom. For months, I sat in a chair, tethered to an oxygen bottle while Rhonda pushed the heavy lawn mower and rolled the big garbage cans to the street. I could only sit and watch as she repaired fences and then hurried inside to prepare our lunch and dinner. I watched as she kept an immaculate count of the handfuls of pills that I took several times a day. She did everything that I was supposed to do and did it on top of everything else.

It took months before I could return to work, even remotely at my home desk, and over a year before I could drive into my office. I had countless doctor visits, but slowly I got better. My need for oxygen got less each month and my handfuls of pills got smaller and smaller. It was slow, but it was steady.

My exact disease was never determined. I eventually went back into the hospital for a procedure to biopsy my lungs, in hopes of learning something from the cellular level. But that also returned nothing helpful. The disease scarred about 40% of my lungs and did damage to my leg muscles.

After I had been home for a few months and was making progress, Rhonda told me about the midnight text and phone call. As she told me, it seemed so incredible, that I instantly started scrolling back on my phone's call logs, I scrolled and scrolled past pages of our calls. I scrolled past the daily encouragement calls from my sisters and brother and friends. I slowed down as I got close to the date. There it was, on April 6 at 12:16 am. A call to Rhonda lasting 3 hours and 42 minutes. I opened my text app and started scrolling past the hundreds of texts that we had shared. I scrolled and scrolled and then stopped the spinning with my thumb. I stared at the phone screen. And there was the text to Rhonda, while I was in the darkest, deepest sleep of my life.

To her and me, it's nothing short of a miracle. To you, it may be something else. But know that not a day goes by that I don't think of those midnight words.

"I love you baby. I'll see you when I wake up well."

* * *

239

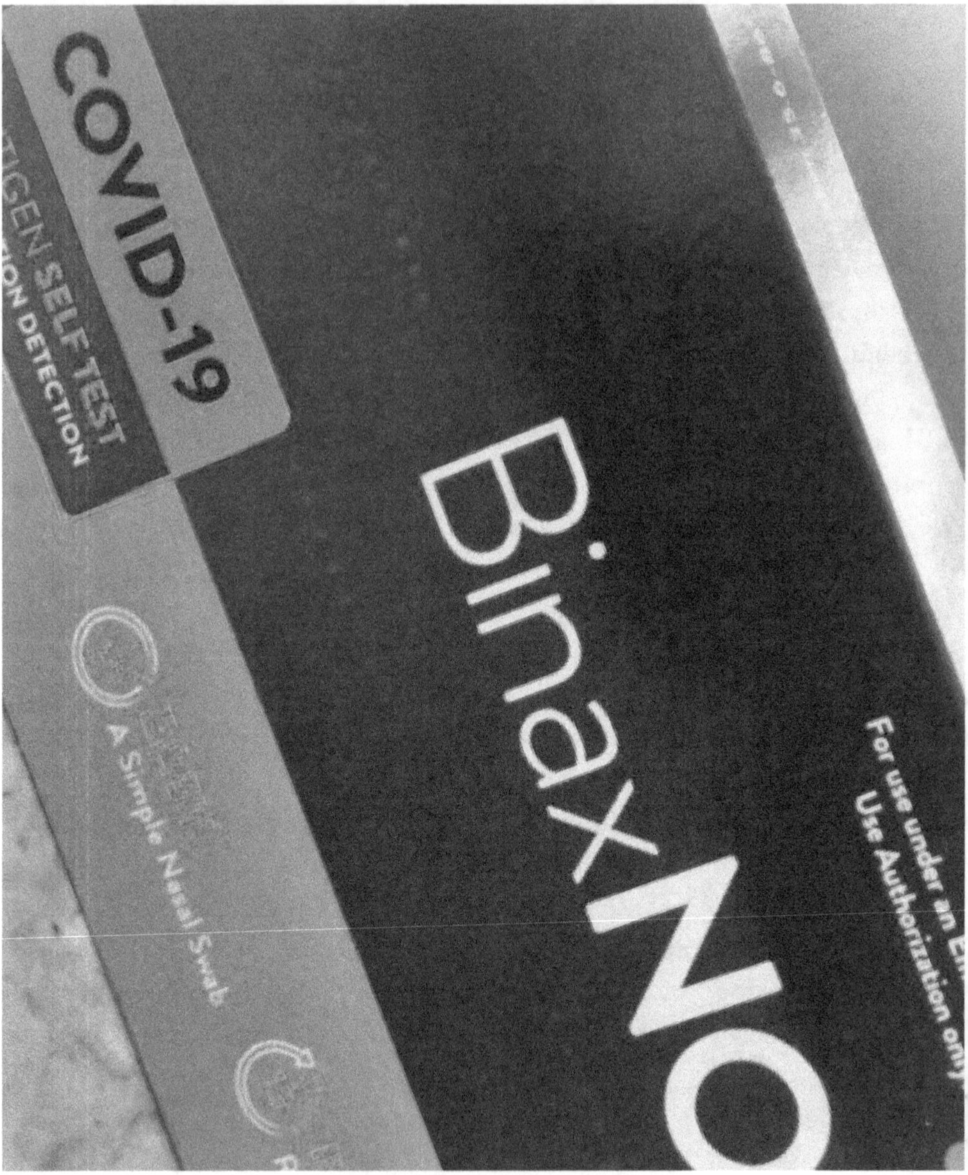
COVID-19
A Simple Nasal Swab
Use Authorization only

HOME TEST

Minutes

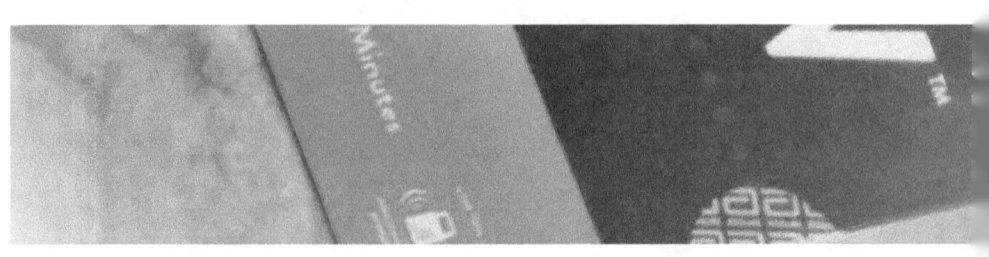

45

HOME TEST

One day when I was in college, I saw my good friend Craig McMullen in the quad and said, "What's up, homeboy?"

He said back, "Not much, home style." So, for the next week or so, we greeted each other with every connotation of home... Home cookin', home plate, home school, hometown, Home Depot, home decor, home study, home grown, home owner... We eventually exploited them all.

A week later, after we had given up and undoubtedly moved on to something even more dumb, I ran into him on campus again. He had spent the weekend back home with his folks. As he walked up, I could see a big ole grin on his face.

"What's up, home perm?"

We'd missed one. We busted up laughing.

This all came to my mind recently after I realized there's a new possibility now, thanks to our growing pandemic lexicon.

"What's up, home test?"

* * *

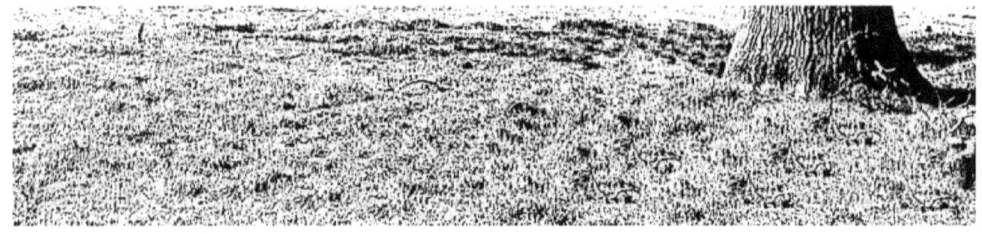

A GLIMPSE INTO OUR FUTURE

46

A GLIMPSE INTO OUR FUTURE

We'd all like to have a crystal ball so that we could get a little peek into our futures. I think that I might have stumbled onto the next best thing. Extreme tiredness!

It seems that these days, everyone I talk to is tired. I must confess that I'm about as routinely tired as I've ever been. I work 12+ hrs a day and 6 days a week. I used to work these long hours, then get home and work a few more around our property. Nowadays I get home 12 hours after I left and collapse into my easy chair.

I think that being this beat up and tired is a good indicator of where you're heading in life. It's like a little glimpse into our future. If something hurts when you're this tired, it's probably soon going to feel like that when you're not tired. If you do dumb stuff when you're this tired, then pretty soon you're going to be doing dumb stuff when you're not tired. If what I'm seeing is any indication of where I'm heading, I need to spend my easy chair time on my phone, researching the best rest homes in the area!

Last week I got home after a long and tiring day and decided to take a bath before I collapsed into my chair. I love a nice soothing hot bath. Since I take my glasses off and can't see much, Rhonda takes a Sharpie and prints a big S on the shampoo and a big C on the conditioner.

Well, on this particular day I was worn out. I grabbed a bottle, looked at it, and read "C." My mind said, yep that's it... Champoo. I got some in my hand

and started working it through my hair, but something just wasn't right. I grabbed the bottle for a second look. Yep, C for Champoo.

After about another minute, my tired (but recovering) mind said...wait a minute, there's no such thing as Champoo. This is Conditioner!

To make myself feel better, I told myself that I had simply read it in Spanish (champú). But I knew the truth. My failing mind eventually found the S and then used the C and finished up.

If that's a glimpse into my future, then I'm not liking it much. But it gets worse.

A couple of weeks ago on one particularly long day, I got in my truck and started my 30-minute drive home. I figure that in the past 25 years, I've made the drive about 6000 times. I typically use the time to think and enjoy some music. But on this day, I was a bit zoned out.

I decided to call Rhonda and let her know that I was on my way.

I pushed the button on my steering wheel and said, "Call Rhonda's cell."

The music shut off and the familiar phone lady's voice said, "Rhonda's Cell, please say dial or correction."

So, I said "Dial or correction."

Phone lady came back and said, "Please say, dial or correction."

Again, I did what she instructed and said, "Dial or correction."

Phone lady came back, but this time I perceived some tone in her voice. "Please say dial OR correction!"

This time I responded, "Well dial then! Damn! You don't have to get pissy with me!"

Phone lady responded, "Dialing Pastor Robert."

This put me in a panic.

"Well shit! No! Cancel! Stop! Representative! No!"

I started pushing every button on my steering wheel to try and cancel the call. I even managed to accidentally honk the horn a couple of times.

I finally stopped yelling and pushing buttons and listened. My music came back on. I had canceled the call.

Phew! So, I just gave up on the phone and started listening to my music again.

About a minute later, the music stopped, and phone lady announced over my speakers, "Call from Pastor Robert."

Apparently, the call did go through and hung up. But he got the "missed call" notification.

This time I managed to hit the decline button. The very last thing I wanted at that moment was to try to explain to Pastor Robert that I really didn't intend to make the call and that it happened because I was having a tiff with my phone voice lady and that she was just trying to teach me a lesson.

Well, lesson learned. I will try to be more alert and polite in future conversations with her. I don't want any trouble. I can just imagine the next time she and I get in a spat, hearing her say, "Dialing Aged Oaks Retirement Home, patient admitting department."

* * *

LIFE IS...

47

LIFE IS...

When I got home from the hospital after being sick, Rhonda had ordered a special chair for me to sit in while I recovered. When we pulled into the driveway, it took everything I had and everything she had, to get me and my oxygen bottle, out of the car seat, down the driveway, across the yard, through the front door, and to the chair. It was the longest distance I had walked in weeks.

I leaned into the new gray chair, pushed the recline button and settled back. It was a happy moment. I was home and I wasn't dead. Everything is relative, but at that moment, it seemed like the greatest day in my life.

The new chair was in the living room, facing the TV on the wall. I could look to the left and see Rhonda cooking in the open kitchen. I could look to the right and see our green backyard and shady trees through the big glass door. For that moment, it was perfect.

For the next month or so, I lived in that chair, tethered to an oxygen generator, by a long green hose. The oxygen machine made a soothing white noise, churning out oxygen, 24 hours a day.

Twice a day, I took handfuls of pills that Rhonda carefully counted out. Big ones, little ones, tablets, and capsules. They were all slowly saving my life. But the pills brought their own set of problems. One of those pills, for whatever good it was doing, was also making sure that I rarely slept. I napped off and on during the day, but I was awake all night. Every night.

When everyone else in the world is asleep and the house and world are both silent, you can't help but think. It would only take one hint of something, maybe a picture on my phone, and I would cascade into hours of thought. That cafe in Barcelona. That hot night in Mexico. My cannonball off our deck into that cool ocean water in Panama. My idle mind just looked for something to think about. The time that I plucked a tomato worm and accidentally tossed it on our daughter Teresa. The old truck that my son and I had restored and painted like an American flag. I never ran out of memories to think about during the seemingly endless supply of nighttime hours and solitude.

The inside of our little house is beautiful. Rhonda has decorated the dining room and living room with fun little conversation pieces, like a 1920s Kodak camera, antique locks and keys and an old wall clock. Inspirational wall art is scattered around the other pieces on the walls. Each piece was tastefully and painstakingly hung in just the right spot. A quarter of an inch left or right, and it wouldn't be perfect.

When my big recovery chair was delivered, Rhonda unboxed it and put it together by herself. I'm sure she moved the furniture around here and there, until she found the perfect spot. Again, a quarter of an inch left or right would not do. Perfect.

Some nights as I sat in the silence, I'd read the words on the hanging wall art. Important and beautiful words. *LOVE IS THE MASTER KEY THAT OPENS THE GATES OF HAPPINESS. LIVE TO THE FULLEST. BREAK THE RULES. FORGIVE QUICKLY. KISS SLOWLY. LOVE TRULY. LAUGH UNCONTROLLABLY. NEVER FORGET ANYTHING THAT MADE YOU SMILE.*

Late one night, as I sat and looked around the room, I realized that Rhonda had truly found the perfect spot for my chair. Yes, I could see her in the kitchen, and I could see the outside through the glass door. But also from that particular spot, a portion of a sign in the kitchen was blocked from my view by a pillar that she and I had built during our kitchen remodel. From my perfect spot, all that I could see of the sign was LIFE IS. The rest of the sign was hidden.

Of course, I knew the word that was hidden. I had seen the sign a million times. But in that moment in the middle of the night, seeing it half-covered by a pillar, made me think. Life is... what?

Now the thought was wide open. I wondered, what if I was making that sign, what would I print?

Perhaps I'd print that LIFE IS UNPREDICTABLE? That one was too easy. Six weeks before that moment, I was a walking and talking tough guy. But there I lay, barely able to walk, and connected to an oxygen hose. One moment I was waltzing through life, the next moment I was in a hospital and on a ventilator, with doctors telling my Rhonda not to get her hopes up too high. Yes, life is unpredictable. But that's depressing. That's not what I would put on a sign.

How about LIFE IS NOT FAIR?

During those dark nights, I spent way too much time being angry about life's injustice. Why me? Why did this happen? What did I do to deserve this? In the morning, I'd often share my anger with Rhonda. I was fortunate that she had a soothing, but definitive response. "Listen Rawge, bad things sometimes happen to good people. It was not your fault. You didn't do anything wrong. Find something else to think about. There is no good in anger. Period."

She was right. So that wouldn't be my sign.

So maybe my sign would say that LIFE IS BEAUTIFUL. Maybe I would simply print LIFE IS WORK. Perhaps I'd just say LIFE IS ABUNDANT. As I conjured up every new possibility, I'd follow each of them with some long thoughts on what the statement meant.

After a week or so of thinking and dwelling on such a simple question, I realized that none of the signs I thought about could capture life. Life is ours to create. Life is what we make of it. The good, the bad, and the in between. We can choose how we fill in that important question. Even laying in my chair in the dark, I realized that I had power. I could choose how to fill in the sign. I could choose how to define my life.

I wouldn't change a thing about the half-hidden sign in the kitchen. Rhonda had set me up in the perfect spot. The obscured message had managed to reveal way more to me than the full message ever could.

Life Is...

* * *

CANARY IN THE COAL MINE

Rawge

48

CANARY IN THE COAL MINE

When I was a kid, we lived out in the middle of nowhere. But once in a while, we'd travel to a big city, with names like Hanford and Bakersfield and Fresno. In these places, we'd get to sit down and eat in a restaurant. At home we ate fried chicken and mashed potatoes, but our rare trips to a restaurant allowed us to eat shrimp and chow mein and big juicy hamburgers with salty french fries. Sometimes we kids would even get turned loose in a mall. On these glorious days, I'd head straight to the music store and the pet store.

In the music store, I'd walk around and stare at the beautiful instruments. I'd drool at the shiny new electric guitars and the chrome-like harmonicas. I could stare at the rows of banjos and mandolins and dream that I could get one someday. If the store wasn't crowded and the salesman was having a good day, sometimes he'd let me sit at a piano or an organ and play Chopsticks with my two fingers. But even with aisles and aisles of beautiful wood and strings, before long, I'd head for the pet store.

There I would walk the aisles of big lizards and snakes. I would marvel at all the pretty greens and checks and bands. Next, I'd skip past the puppies and cats and get over to the fish and big aquariums. There were fish of every color. I wondered if there were that many fish in the aquariums, then how many must be in the big ocean? Next, I'd skip past some of the more exotic animals, since I already had a monkey and an alligator. Eventually I would find myself in my favorite area. The birds.

The section was always noisy, with parrots and parakeets and cockatoos and cockatiels, all squawking at once. But even through the din of sound, I can remember the first time I heard a canary sing. It was the most beautiful thing I had ever heard and instantly I wanted one! So, for the next year, I made it my mission to get one. At every opportunity, I pleaded with my parents to buy one for me. Birthday? I want a canary. Christmas? I want a canary. I even tried the nontraditional gifting holidays. Arbor day? Canary! First day of summer? Canary! A tooth under my pillow? I just want a canary!

Well, I never got a canary, but it wasn't for lack of pleading. A few years later, I was even more fascinated by them when I learned that coal miners kept them in their tunnels as gas monitors. While the miners worked, they listened to the canaries sing. If the yellow birds stopped singing, someone would run to the cage to see if they had died. If the tiny canaries were dead, then it meant it was only a matter of time before the 200-pound miners would succumb to the same fate. So at that morbid sign, the big miners dropped whatever they were doing and ran pell-mell to the nearest exit.

Ever since 2020, when I got deathly sick and spent over a month in a hospital, I've often wondered, what was my dead canary in the coal mine moment? If I'd have finally gotten a canary and trained it to ride on my shoulder, pirate style, what was that moment when it fell over dead? I still find myself looking at things and wondering what tried to kill me. What did I innocently and unknowingly breathe in, that eventually sent me to the hospital on a ventilator and scarred my lungs forever? Was I in our backyard when the canary died? Was I at work, walking through one of our forests? Was I sitting in a restaurant, laughing with friends?

Well, there are a couple of points to all of this. We don't have a canary on our shoulders to warn us of health conditions. But we can all be vigilant to our bodies and our health. We are our own canaries. One thing I've learned is that in the coal mines, once the canary died, no miner decided to be a tough guy and say, "I'll wait and see what happens." None of them said, "I'll give it one more day, I'm sure it will be better by then." Nope. The strongest of men ran for the exit.

But that's what I did. When Rhonda pleaded for me to go to the hospital, I said maybe tomorrow, if it's not better. Then another day, and then another day. Granted I had a doctor telling me that she was sure it was Covid. There was no cure, so going to the ER would only put others at risk. But I shouldn't have waited. I knew. In fact, when I finally let Rhonda take me to the walk-up triage area and they hurriedly put me in the ambulance to take me to a hospital, I asked the paramedics to please take me to a specific hospital nearer to my home. They responded that I probably wouldn't make it that far! The rest is history. I'm sure that had they started the tests and ultimate treatment a few days earlier, I wouldn't be handicapped for life.

So, friends, we don't have a canary. We only have our own senses. When you're sick, don't be a tough guy or gal.

Don't be a Rawge.

Like the miners in the shafts knew, time is critical.

Don't hesitate.

Take care of yourselves!

* * *

THE GOOD OLD DAYS

49

THE GOOD OLD DAYS!

I was scrolling Facebook the other day and saw a meme. There are always a million memes, so I scrolled past. But after I saw it a few more times, I read through it. If I saw it three times, it must be on people's minds. I like having my finger on the pulse of the community.

The gist of the meme was how sad it is that we've raised our kids for a world that no longer exists. The thought was that this generation is somehow not as good as the previous generation. The world is going to hell. If we could just roll back to the good old days. I'm sure my parents thought the same thing. And their parents and their parents, and their parents, and so on. If we could just freeze time, the world would be a better place.

I disagree. I wonder, if we rolled back and froze time in a generation, which generation would we choose?

Would we go way back to when the adults spent all day trying to find food, and then all night trying not to be food. I'm glad we didn't freeze time there.

What if we only went back to our great-grandparents' time? Three out of every ten babies died before their first birthday. Few people lived past 50 years old. And worst of all, rich white people could own black people. I'm certainly glad that we didn't stall in those "good old days."

Maybe we could go back to the turn of the last century when our grandparents were born? Women couldn't vote. If you got any infection, you'd likely die, as even penicillin hadn't been discovered yet. If you weren't a white male, then you were a second-class citizen. Again, I'm glad we didn't decide to freeze our country during that time.

How about our parents' time. I'm sure that they lamented that the world was going to hell in a handbasket. In fact, I heard mine say it a few times. Back then, every boss in every company was a white man and he could slap his secretary on the ass any time he felt like it. People could stand around the water cooler and tell racist and dirty jokes. Black people had to enter stores through a back door, if they were allowed at all, and had to be off the streets before the sun went down. Cars were beautiful, but if you wrecked, you died. Yep, I'm glad our world didn't pull a freeze-frame back then.

So, I guess it's true, that each generation raised their kids for a world that no longer existed. But I won't fret about that. I'd rather put my effort into leaving them a world that's better than I found it. Maybe this generation can leave a world where everyone, no matter of sex, age, creed, or color, can have the exact same opportunities as me. Perhaps a world where a child who's born differently won't have to hide it and be shunned in the halls of their high school or the pews of their church. We could leave a world where if you actually lived your life asking WWJD, you wouldn't be called woke for doing so.

But I think the part that makes people sad is the really good parts of each generation that seem to have been lost. There are plenty of things that I think we could fight harder to hold onto. Things like families having dinner together every night and talking and laughing. People growing gardens and eating fresh vegetables. Kids with time to explore and play in a safe neighborhood. Fresh air that you didn't have to drive a hundred miles up in the mountains to find. Oh, and kites. I miss kites.

I'm sure that bringing back big car tailfins is too much to ask, but it's worth trying.

* * *

THE GOOD OLD DAYS!

LEARNING FROM THE "AIN'TS"

50

LEARNING FROM THE "AIN'TS"

You might remember the line from my favorite movie, *Oh Brother Where Art Thou?* where the politician Homer Stokes asks, "Is you is, or is you ain't, my constituency?"

We jokingly ask that around our house, about random things. "Is you is, or is you ain't, going to the store?" "Is you is, or is you ain't, ready for dinner?" It's just fun to say.

But as dumb as it sounds, there's some value to the question, "Is you is, or is you ain't?" Often in my life, as I've grappled to understand what something *is*, I've first learned what something *ain't*. After a process of ticking off the *ain'ts*, I can better start to understand the *is*.

Since I was young, I've wrestled with what it is to be a Christian. Well, during the past few years, I've learned a lot about what it *ain't*. That's been helpful.

What is a patriot? Well, in the last few years, and certainly during some weeks in January 2021, I've learned what it *ain't*. That's been helpful.

But like most every person on Earth, I've spent some time wondering, "What is the meaning of life? Why are we here? Why am I here?"

I've watched billionaires die, and not take a penny with them. So, it *ain't* to get rich and accumulate wealth. That's helpful.

I've known people who have died from years of job stress. So, I know it *ain't* to work my life away. That's helpful.

I know of people who had big megaphones and spent their lives being loud and mean and got a lot of attention. A week after they died, no one even mentions their names. So, I know it *ain't* to be loud and mean and scream for attention. That's helpful

So, I've checked off a bunch of *ain'ts* about why am I here? But I've still got questions. Since a couple years ago, when I almost died, I more often ask myself, "Why am I *STILL* here?"

But I'm getting it figured out. I get a little closer to the answer every time I look into Rhonda's blue eyes. I get closer every time one of the grand-kids runs up yelling, "Papa!" Or every time I see the smile on someone's face that just got 'em a free guitar from my shop. Or every time I watch another sunrise.

Yep, I'm getting it figured out.

* * *

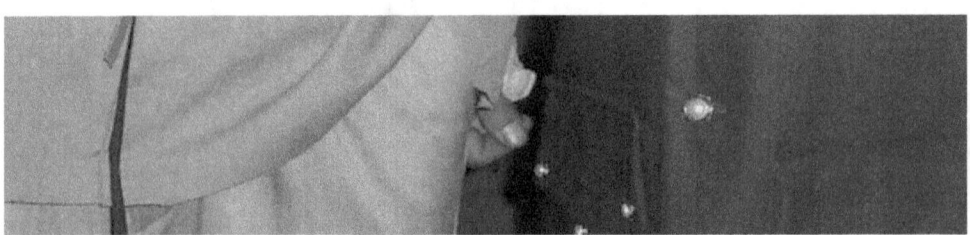

ROYALTY

51

ROYALTY

By now, most of us have shelled out the hundred bucks, swabbed our mouth, and sent the package off to learn about where we came from. There's something exciting about seeing a chart showing our ancestral roots. We all hope that we'll learn something new. Maybe we'll learn that our distant ancestors came from some exotic place. Maybe we'll learn why we love Celtic music or that we've got family that we've never met. Most of it is fun, but probably not very useful, unless of course you learn something startling.

I'm pretty sure that there's royalty buried somewhere in my family tree. I'm just waiting for that hundred buck test to prove it true.

Last week I asked Rhonda to throw away one of my nicer shirts. I told her that something in the collar irritated my neck. I pulled the collar to the side and showed her a red mark.

Before she tossed it, Rhonda put on her glasses and inspected the collar. She ran her sensitive fingertips over it and found that tiny piece of annoying thread, no bigger than an eyelash, sticking up from a seam. She removed it, and now it's fine. That tiny piece of thread was driving me crazy!

Do you remember the tale *The Princess and the Pea*? A prince was wanting to marry a young lady who claimed to be a princess. To prove her nobility, the tale says that the queen had the would-be princess sleep on a bed on top of twenty feather mattresses. The queen secretly placed a pea beneath the bottom mattress. The next day, when the princess complained of a horrible night's sleep because of a lump in the mattress, she was proven to be of noble descent. She even showed a bruise on her back. Only royalty could be so sensitive!

So, there it is. I must be noble. The tiniest things can irritate me. I'm just waiting for all of the DNA background to come together, and I'll surely get notified by a distant relative informing me of my lost nobility.

OK, I didn't write the funny tale of *The Princess and the Pea.* Hans Christian Anderson wrote it 200 years ago. If I had written it, I'd have said that our nobility is proven if we are happy, peaceful, patient, kind, good, faithful, gentle, and self-controlled. I read that somewhere.

But that's not funny or fun. So, I'll keep scratching my neck and complaining that there's an eyelash stuck in my shirt, while I wait for a crown to show up in the mail. Why just last week, I got an email from a Nigerian prince who apparently is a relative of mine and wants to send me a lot of money. We're working out the details now!!!

* * *

ROYALTY

THANK YOU CARDS

52

THANK YOU CARDS

Back in 2017, after one of our Roots Gospel Jam concerts, someone left a card on the stage, and it was addressed to me. I picked it up and stuck it in my back pocket.

It was 10 o'clock at night and I was hot and tired, but I felt that we had just performed one of our particularly better concerts. Everyone in the group was extremely talented and always did well. But on this evening, I felt that even I had played and sang about as good as ever. Besides leading the songs, I was the *between songs* entertainment. I told jokes and stories and got the audience involved. Much of my jokes and humor was about me making fun of myself. That was my favorite part and people loved it.

When we got everything packed up and finally got home for the night, I was excited to open the card. I was sure that it was some kind of thank you for the fun evening of raucous music, bucolic bonhomie and big plates of homemade BBQ and coleslaw. Rhonda always prepared a delicious meal, and it was always free for everyone, sometimes two or three hundred of them. I opened the card with some anticipation. But oddly, the card was one of those "Get better soon" cards. I thought, hmmm... I'm not sick.

Inside the card, someone had written... *Rawge, we hope you get better soon. Seriously. Practice might be the answer. Get better!*

* * *

NEW YEAR'S RESOLUTIONS

53

NEW YEAR'S RESOLUTIONS

I t's December 31, 2022. Another year has passed and a new one lays before me. After 62 of them came and went, it seems a little cliche to sit and ponder on the past one and plan how I'll make the next one better. But that's what I do. I do it and label it as my "New Year's Resolutions." I do it every year.

During those 62 years, I've already gone through all the classics. You know the ones...losing weight, getting more organized and saving money. Those never panned out. But about 10 years ago, I decided on one that was very simple. It was so simple, even a dog could attempt it, and if it worked out, it'd be good for everyone around me. I've kept this resolution and renewed it each year.

Less Barkin' and More Waggin'!

As simple as it sounds, it's a tough one. There are a million things every day that make me want to bark. There's a never-ending supply of people who make me want to growl. There are days when it seems like there's not much to wag about. So, I've failed my resolution a lot.

But I've tried and I'll try again this year.

I once read that to be successful in keeping your resolutions, you need to write them down and then share them with others. That will keep you honest. So, there it is friends. Now, if you ever hear me backsliding, feel free to give me a quick check.

Hey Rawge! Less Barkin'! More Waggin'!
Happy New Year friends!

* * *

THOUGHTS AND PRAYERS

54

THOUGHTS AND PRAYERS

Dear friends. I want to take a moment to ask you all for thoughts and prayers for my dear Rhonda. She is having a rough time right now and I'm concerned.

She is really struggling with my immaturity!

She didn't even respond with a laughing emoji when I texted her this pic and said "Hey baby, look what I saw in the gas station bathroom!

This was our conversation when I got back to the car.

"Hey baby, did you get my text?"

"Yes."

"Wasn't it funny?"

"It was stupid. You're so childish! You need to grow up and start acting your age."

"OK. When I'm 69!"

"Agh!"

* * *

CARICATURE

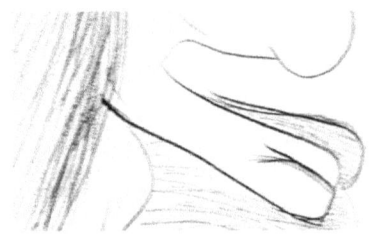
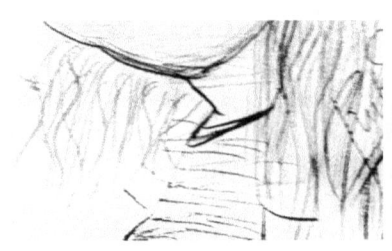

55

CARICATURE

We live in a world of selfies and glamour filters. I appreciate that I can hold my phone at arm's length, push a button, and I get a picture that makes me look twenty years younger. I'm vain. I've got wrinkles. I've gained some pounds. I don't want to see the real me. I don't want truth.

Don't ever ask for a street artist caricature unless you're ready for the truth! If you can't handle the truth, then you're better off going with the selfie stick and the glamour filters. Caricature artists look deep and then don't hold anything back. If it's big, then it gets bigger. If it's round, then it gets rounder. If it sags, then it gets saggier. That's just how it works. A caricature is the real you.

We've had these done a few times over the years, including on our honeymoon. We tried it again recently.

Here's the assessment.

Apparently, I'm the love child of Jay Leno and Sarah Jessica Parker, and Rhonda is here for the cross-dresser's convention.

* * *

FREE ADVICE

56

FREE ADVICE

This is the last chapter. Almost everything I have written has had some kind of moral to the story, even if the moral is simply to not do stupid stuff like I did. I started writing these stories right after I was sick when I couldn't do much besides sit. I'm finishing this last chapter, sitting on a deck over the water, on a little island outside of Bocas Del Toro, Panama. Rhonda and I have been here for a month.

I started writing by making a list of the stories I wanted to tell and what I'd like for people to know about me. Originally, I thought I could complete it in a year. Some part of the writing was just a challenge to myself, to still be alive in another year. Part of me probably thought that if things turned bad again, I could just say, "I can't die now, I haven't finished my book yet!"

My one-year project has turned into three. It started in a convalescent recliner in my living room and ended on a chaise lounge in Panama. But as surprising as it may seem, I got pretty busy. I'm back to working full-time. Rhonda and I are back to playing music on Sundays. And I'm still a full-time trophy husband. It's a participation trophy, but still.

During my three years of writing, I've shared excerpts with friends and on social media. I've thoroughly enjoyed all of the comments, good and otherwise. But one comment stuck out. Early on, a friend posted about one of my stories, "Thanks Rawge. Good Advice!"

Well, drat! I thought I had camouflaged the advice part better. Dang it! I had hoped that if there was anything that actually fell into the advice category, it would be better hidden under encouragement or an earnest opportunity to learn from my mistakes. But I guess the only thing buried beneath it all was my innate zeal for giving free advice.

I think free advice is just part of my generous nature. I'm so generous that I'll give advice even before anyone asks for it. I know that the whole world loves free and unsolicited advice.

Back when we did our Roots Gospel Jam concerts, I would give free preaching advice to the pastors of whatever church would host us. It was always good advice. I remember telling one pastor that the key to a great sermon is to have a powerful beginning and a powerful ending, and to keep the two as close together as possible!!! Well, it got a good laugh, and I've given that advice a number of times. But I don't think a single preacher ever took me up on it.

To finish up my book, I sat and thought about all the free advice I've dispensed in my life. I'm sure it's an embarrassing amount. I'm also sure that I've advised about everything from love to health, and from careers to relationships. I'm pretty sure that I've doled out advice on stuff I didn't even know anything about, just making it up as I went along. But best of all, I'm absolutely sure there are people all over the world, strolling down the easy road of life, all because I jumped in without asking and shared my sage advice. Yep, I'm sure of it.

As I sat and wondered whether or not any of my advice was ever actually helpful, I thought I would end my book by trying to recall the best advice I've ever given. I had to think about it a bit and amble through some memories, but I think I've got it. It was about twenty years ago, and I gave it to a seventeen-year-old boy. Teenage boys need advice. I know for a fact that this kid took the advice and I also know for a fact that it saved his life! Well, if it didn't save his life, I guarantee you it saved him from a serious ass-whoopin'.

My advice to the kid was a simple few words.

"Listen boy, keep your hands off my daughter."

He listened. He lived. I stayed out of prison. Sometimes my advice does as much for me as it does for someone else.

I hope that buried within my true stories there was some kernel of "advice" that made your day easier, or sunnier, or at least added a bit of laughter. I hope that woven through all of them was the simple message that we're all supposed to love and be kind to one another. Now, that's good advice!

* * *